Biomes Atlases

DESERTS
AND SEMI-DESERTS

Michael Allaby, Robert Anderson and Ian Crofton

Raintree

www.raintreepublishers.co.uk

Phone 44 (0) 1865 888112
Send a fax to 44 (0) 1865 314091
Visit the Raintree bookshop online at www.raintreepublishers.co.uk
to browse our catalogue and order online.

First published in Great Britain in 2003 by Raintree, Halley Court,
Jordan Hill, Oxford, OX2 8EJ, part of Harcourt Education Ltd.
Raintree is a registered trademark of Harcourt Education Ltd.
Copyright © 2002 The Brown Reference Group plc.

The moral right of the proprieter has been asserted.

Printed and bound in Singapore.

ISBN 1 844 21149 5
07 06 05 04 03
10 9 8 7 6 5 4 3 2 1

British Library Cataloging-in-Publication Data

A full catalogue is available for this book from the British Library.

The Brown Reference Group plc
Project Editor: Ben Morgan
Deputy Editor: Dr. Rob Houston
Copy-editors: John Farndon and Angela Koo
Consultant: Dr. Mark Hostetler, Department
    of Wildlife Ecology and Conservation,
    University of Florida
Designer: Reg Cox
Cartographers: Mark Walker and
    Darren Awuah
Picture Researcher: Clare Newman
Indexer: Kay Ollerenshaw
Managing Editor: Bridget Giles
Design Manager: Lynne Ross
Production: Alastair Gourlay

Raintree Publishers
Editors: Isabel Thomas and Kate Buckingham

Front cover: Dunes in the Namib Desert,
southern Africa.
Inset: Fennec, a type of desert fox.

Title page: Death Valley, California.

The acknowledgments on p. 64 form
part of this copyright page. Every effort has
been made to contact copyright holders of
any material reproduced in this book. Any
omissions will be rectified in subsequent
printings if notice is given to the publishers.

About this book

The introductory pages of this book describe the biomes of the world and then the desert biome. The five main chapters look at different aspects of deserts: climate, plants, animals, people and future. Between the chapters are detailed maps that focus on famous or important deserts. The map pages are shown in the contents in italics, **like this**.

Throughout the book you'll also find boxed stories or fact files about deserts. The icons here show what the boxes are about. At the end of the book is a glossary, which explains what all the difficult words mean. After the glossary is a list of books and websites for further research and an index, allowing you to find subjects anywhere in the book.

 Climate

 People

 Plants

 Future

 Animals

 Facts

Contents

Biomes of the world 4

Deserts of the world 6

Sonoran Desert 8

Desert climates 10

Atacama 18

Desert plants 20

Kalahari and Namib 30

Desert animals 32

Sahara 42

People and the desert 44

Gobi and Takla Makan 54

The future for deserts 56

Glossary 62

Further research 63

Index 64

Biomes of the world

Biologists divide the living world into major zones called biomes. Each biome has its own distinctive climate, plants and animals.

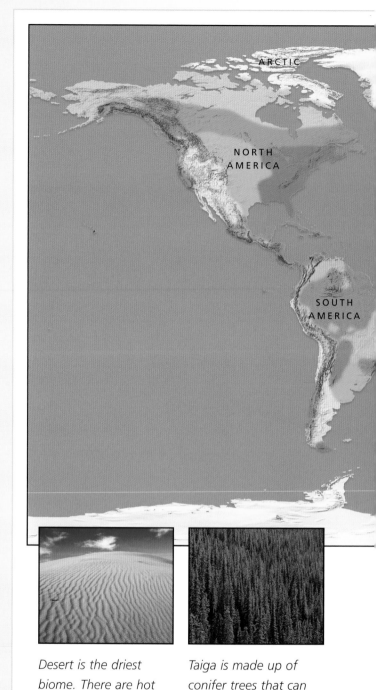

Desert is the driest biome. There are hot deserts and cold ones.

Taiga is made up of conifer trees that can survive freezing winters.

If you were to walk all the way from the north of Canada to the Amazon **rainforest**, you'd notice the wilderness changing dramatically along the way.

Northern Canada is a freezing and barren place without trees, where only tiny brownish-green plants can survive in the icy ground. But trudge south for long enough and you enter a magical world of conifer forests, where moose, caribou (reindeer) and wolves live. After several weeks, the conifers disappear, and you reach the grass-covered **prairies** of the central USA. The further south you go, the drier the land gets and the hotter the sun feels, until you find yourself hiking through a cactus-filled **desert**. But once you reach southern Mexico, the cacti start to disappear, and strange **tropical** trees begin to take their place. Here, the muggy air is filled with the calls of exotic birds and the drone of tropical insects. Finally, in Colombia you cross the Andes mountain range – whose chilly peaks remind you a little of your starting point – and descend into the dense, swampy jungles of the Amazon rainforest.

Scientists have a special name for the different regions – such as desert, tropical rainforest and prairie – that you'd pass through on such a journey. They call them **biomes**. Everywhere on Earth can be classified as being in one biome or another, and the same biome often appears in lots of

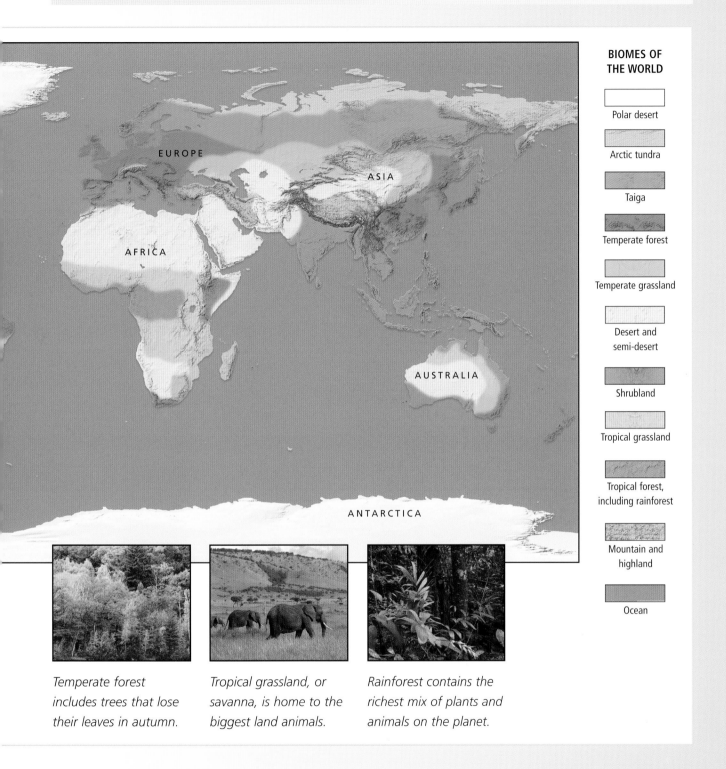

BIOMES OF
THE WORLD

Polar desert

Arctic tundra

Taiga

Temperate forest

Temperate grassland

Desert and
semi-desert

Shrubland

Tropical grassland

Tropical forest,
including rainforest

Mountain and
highland

Ocean

EUROPE

ASIA

AFRICA

AUSTRALIA

ANTARCTICA

*Temperate forest
includes trees that lose
their leaves in autumn.*

*Tropical grassland, or
savanna, is home to the
biggest land animals.*

*Rainforest contains the
richest mix of plants and
animals on the planet.*

different places. For instance, there are areas of rainforest as far apart as Brazil, Africa and South-east Asia. Although the plants and animals that inhabit these forests are different, they live in similar ways. Likewise, the prairies of North America are part of the grassland biome, which also occurs in China, Australia and Argentina. Wherever there are grasslands, there are grazing animals that feed on the grass, as well as large carnivores that hunt and kill the grazers.

The map on this page shows how the world's major biomes fit together to make up the biosphere – the zone of life on Earth.

Deserts of the world

There are deserts on every continent, from the sun-baked heart of Africa to the chilly plains of northern China. Together, deserts make up one of Earth's largest biomes.

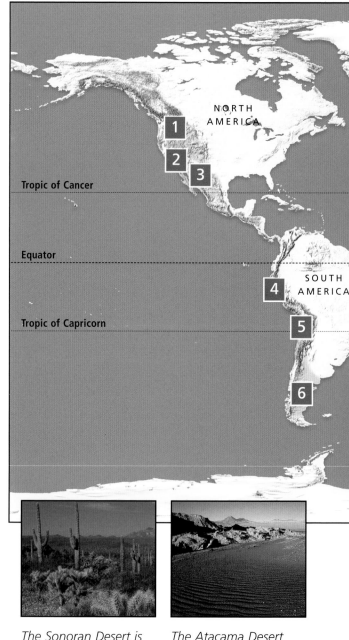

The Sonoran Desert is full of cacti. Flowers often appear in spring.

The Atacama Desert in Chile is the driest place in the world.

Deserts come in all shapes and sizes. Some are tiny, such as the desert of Almería in south-east Spain, but others are huge. The vast **arid** (dry) area that spreads across North Africa, the Arabian peninsula and western Asia is really one gigantic desert, though we give different names to different parts of it.

The world's major deserts lie in two bands near the tropics of **Cancer** and **Capricorn** (two imaginary circles around the planet, north and south of the **equator**). There are also deserts near the poles – Greenland and Antarctica are part of a biome called polar desert. You can find out more about them in the *Arctic Tundra and Polar Deserts* book.

Like most biomes, deserts do not generally have definite boundaries, except where they meet the sea or a major mountain range. In many places they merge gradually into another land biome, such as **shrubland**.

The land near the edge of the desert, which is not quite desert and not quite shrubland, is known as **semi-desert**.

The word desert conjures up images of rolling sand dunes or plains covered in rubble, but not all deserts are like that. Parts of North America's Great Basin, for

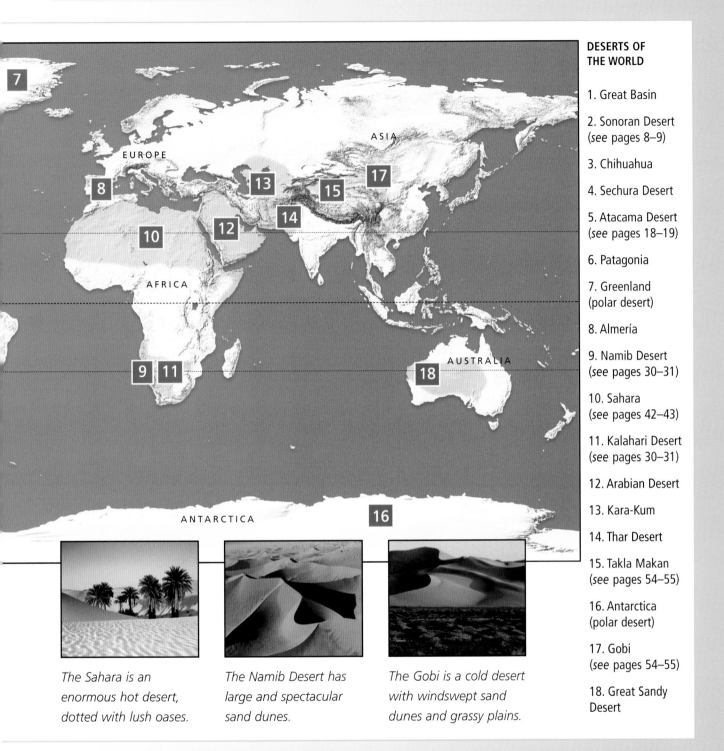

DESERTS OF THE WORLD

1. Great Basin

2. Sonoran Desert (*see* pages 8–9)

3. Chihuahua

4. Sechura Desert

5. Atacama Desert (*see* pages 18–19)

6. Patagonia

7. Greenland (polar desert)

8. Almería

9. Namib Desert (*see* pages 30–31)

10. Sahara (*see* pages 42–43)

11. Kalahari Desert (*see* pages 30–31)

12. Arabian Desert

13. Kara-Kum

14. Thar Desert

15. Takla Makan (*see* pages 54–55)

16. Antarctica (polar desert)

17. Gobi (*see* pages 54–55)

18. Great Sandy Desert

The Sahara is an enormous hot desert, dotted with lush oases.

The Namib Desert has large and spectacular sand dunes.

The Gobi is a cold desert with windswept sand dunes and grassy plains.

instance, are completely flat and glittering white, thanks to a coating of salt crystals. The Sonoran Desert in Arizona is sometimes carpeted with colourful flowers, though only for a short time. Yet, despite their many differences, all deserts do have one thing in common: water is in very short supply.

Most biomes exist because of a distinctive pattern of weather through the year. We call these weather patterns **climates**. Tropical rainforests have a warm and wet climate, for example, while deserts have a very dry climate. So, to understand the desert biome, we need to look first at the desert climate.

Sonoran Desert

6

The Sonoran Desert sprawls across the south-west USA into northern Mexico. It is the hottest North American desert but also the greenest, with forests of giant cacti.

 ## Sonoran facts

▲ Towering saguaro cacti and organ-pipe cacti are the most distinctive plants of this desert.

▲ Summer rain and winter storms often soak the ground, nourishing the many plants.

▲ The Apache chieftain Geronimo (1829–1909) used the Sonoran Desert as a hideaway during a conflict with US forces in the 19th century.

1. Mojave Desert
North of the Sonoran Desert is the Mojave Desert, home of the famously gnarled Joshua trees.

2. Colorado River
This river flows from the Rocky Mountains to Mexico, via the Grand Canyon and Sonoran Desert. The cities of Los Angeles and Phoenix get their water from the river via an aqueduct.

3. Salton Sea
A saltwater lake, formed from water running off irrigated farmland in the Imperial Valley.

4. Imperial Valley
Thousands of miles of irrigation canals have turned this arid valley into an area of intensively farmed land, able to grow citrus fruits, sugar beet and cotton.

5. Yuma Desert
Sand dunes and low sandy plains dotted with creosote bushes make up this very dry part of the desert.

6. Saguaro National Park
Forests of saguaro cacti cover this beautifully scenic preserve in Arizona.

7. Organ Pipe Cactus National Monument
Organ-pipe cacti, named for their dramatic column shape, dominate this park.

8. Kitt Peak Observatory
Conditions for stargazing are perfect at this mountain-top observatory, which enjoys cloudless skies year round.

9. Gulf of California
The warm waters here provide an important breeding ground for blue and grey whales.

10. Baja California
The mountainous Baja peninsula is sometimes considered an extension of the Sonoran Desert.

11. Sierra Madre
The desert merges into forest in this major mountain range.

Desert monsters

The Sonoran Desert has more than its fair share of dangerous animals, including rattlesnakes, scorpions and gila monsters (left). Gila monsters are the largest lizards in North America, and the only venomous ones. They come out at night to hunt for eggs and small animals, such as mice or baby birds. When they catch a victim, they bite it and hold on. Powerful venom flows through grooves in the gila monster's teeth and into the victim's wound, paralysing it. Fortunately, these lizards seldom bite people.

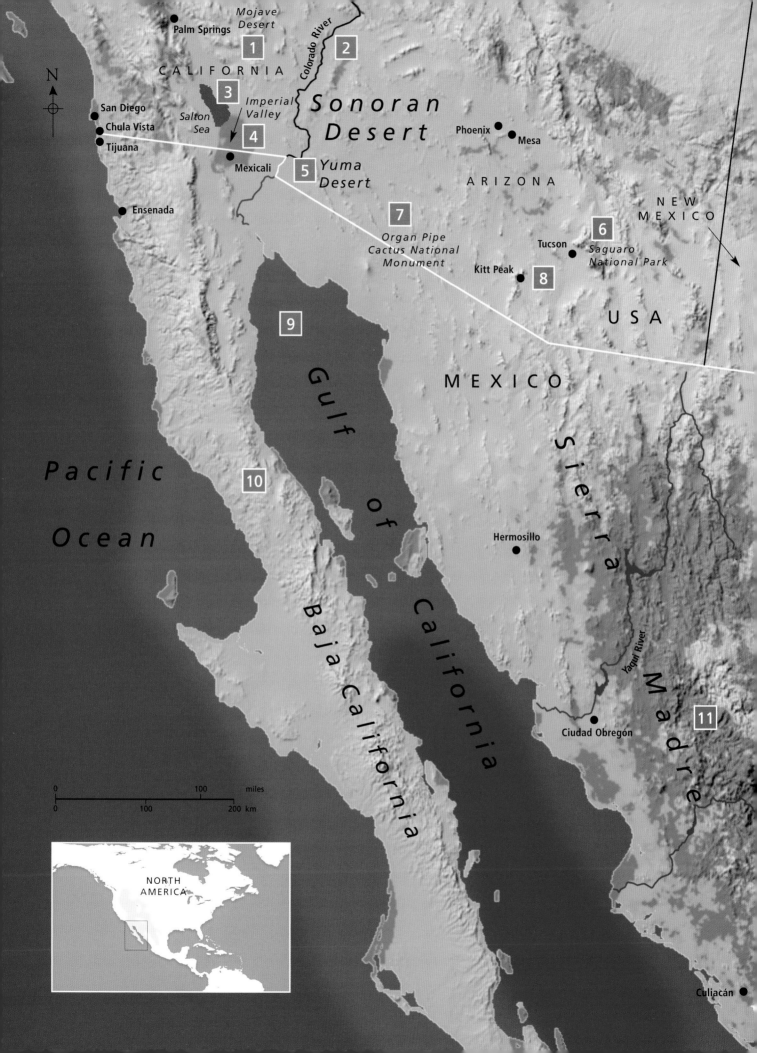

N

Palm Springs

Mojave Desert

Colorado River

1

2

CALIFORNIA

3

Imperial Valley

Salton Sea

San Diego

Chula Vista

Tijuana

4

Mexicali

5

Yuma Desert

**S o n o r a n
D e s e r t**

Phoenix

Mesa

A R I Z O N A

N E W
M E X I C O

Ensenada

7

*Organ Pipe
Cactus National
Monument*

6

Tucson

*Saguaro
National Park*

Kitt Peak

8

U S A

*Pacific

Ocean*

9

10

Gulf

of

California

M E X I C O

Baja California

Hermosillo

S i e r r a

M a d r e

Yaqui River

Ciudad Obregón

11

0   100   miles
0   100   200 km

NORTH
AMERICA

Culiacán

Desert climates

Deserts exist for a very simple reason: lack of rain. But desert climates are surprisingly varied. There are hot deserts, cold deserts, polar deserts, windswept deserts and even deserts covered with fog.

Al Azizia in Libya is probably the hottest place on Earth. On 13 September 1922, the temperature there reached 57.8°C (136°F) – the highest temperature ever recorded. That's really sizzling. The ground there that day would have been hot enough to fry an egg.

Under the burning sun

Al Azizia is in North Africa's Sahara, one of the world's hot deserts. Not all deserts are hot, but the Sahara certainly is. Hot deserts extend all around the world in two belts, to the north and south of the tropical zone around the equator. Further north and south are the cold deserts, and

Even from space, the expanses of sand in the Namib Desert are easily visible. This view is from a satellite looking south.

further still are the ice-covered **polar deserts**.

All deserts are dry, since it is lack of water that makes a desert. They are dry because what little water reaches the desert **evaporates** from the ground and escapes into the **atmosphere**. Intense sunshine and hot, windy weather speed up the evaporation of water from deserts, making them even drier. But how dry is dry? Dictionaries define a desert

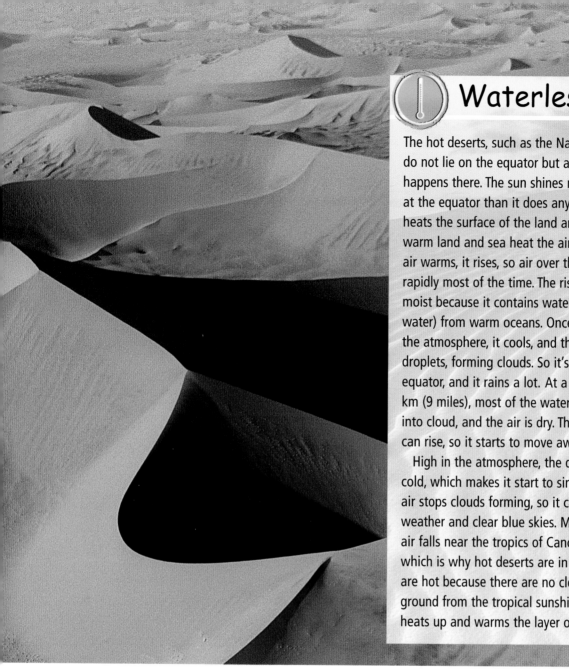

Waterless world

The hot deserts, such as the Namib (pictured here), do not lie on the equator but are created by what happens there. The sun shines more directly all year at the equator than it does anywhere else. This heats the surface of the land and ocean, and the warm land and sea heat the air above them. When air warms, it rises, so air over the equator is rising rapidly most of the time. The rising air is also very moist because it contains water vapour (evaporated water) from warm oceans. Once the air gets high in the atmosphere, it cools, and the vapour turns into droplets, forming clouds. So it's often cloudy at the equator, and it rains a lot. At a height of about 16 km (9 miles), most of the water vapour has turned into cloud, and the air is dry. This is as high as air can rise, so it starts to move away from the equator.

High in the atmosphere, the dry air gets very cold, which makes it start to sink. This sinking dry air stops clouds forming, so it causes dry, sunny weather and clear blue skies. Most of the sinking air falls near the tropics of Cancer and Capricorn, which is why hot deserts are in these regions. They are hot because there are no clouds to shield the ground from the tropical sunshine, so the land heats up and warms the layer of air above it.

as a place that receives less than 250 mm (10 in) of rain a year; for comparison, the city of Aberdeen in Scotland receives about 608 mm (24 in).

Some deserts receive almost no rain at all. In the town of Aswan in southern Egypt, for instance, there are many years when the rainfall is zero. On the rare occasions that it does rain in the desert, the downpour can be torrential. Intense thunderstorms quickly wet the soil surface, then further water just runs off the wet surface in sheets, creating flash floods. In the summer of 1997, heavy rain in the Atlas mountains of Morocco caused

floods that killed more than 250 people. In the same year, floods after rainstorms in north-eastern Iran drowned eleven people.

Although deserts can get very hot during the day, the nights can be bitterly cold. In January, the temperature in the Sahara is high in the early afternoon, but at night it often drops below freezing. That's because dry sand and bare rock heat up quickly when the sun shines on them, but they cool down again just as fast. And because there are no clouds to trap warmth rising from the ground, the heat soon escapes into space once the sun has gone down.

Dust storms and dust devils

Besides being dry, deserts are windy. The ferocious wind blows sand into rolling seas of dunes – it can even wear away solid rock by blasting it with sand. Sometimes the wind blows strongly enough to lift dust and sand into a vast cloud thousands of feet tall. Then it's a dust storm or sandstorm that arrives as a screaming gale, driving dust and fine sand into every corner. People caught in the open can't see and can barely breathe, because the hot air is full of choking grit.

At other times the wind plays tricks. Around the middle of the afternoon, when the ground has been heating for several hours, some places are much hotter than others. Air rising over the hot spots draws in surrounding air and starts to spiral as it rises. If the swirling, dusty air rises only a few feet, it's called a dust devil. But sometimes the swirling air rises much higher – and then it's a whirlwind.

Whirlwinds can be 1.6 km (1 mile) tall. They leap up suddenly and produce howling gusts that are strong enough to smash a wooden hut. During its brief life, a whirlwind wanders about randomly – you can't tell where it will go next. It survives for only a few minutes, but as one dies down, another can leap up nearby. Long ago, before anyone knew what caused whirlwinds, desert peoples were terrified of them. Some people believed God sent whirlwinds as a punishment for sins.

Cold deserts

When we think of deserts, it's the hot, sandy ones that spring to mind. Not all deserts are like this, though. Most of the Sahara and the deserts of Southwest Asia, for example, are covered by bare rock and gravel; the wind blows away the dust and sand. Neither are all deserts hot. The city of Hohhot in China lies on the edge of the Gobi desert. In January the temperature here averages a bitterly cold –13°C (8.6°F), and in July – the warmest month – it barely rises above room temperature. Straddling the border between Mongolia and China, the Gobi looks fairly small on a map showing the whole of Europe and Asia. In fact, it is about 1600 km (1000 miles) from west to east. To its west is another great desert, the Takla Makan, which is about 970 km (600 miles) across.

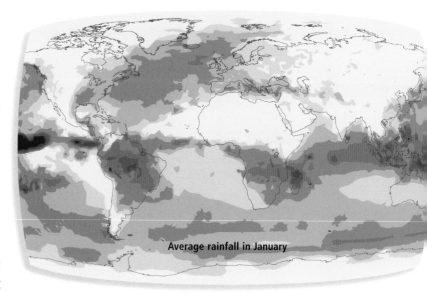

Average rainfall in January

Dark blue in these maps shows areas of rain. Deserts are pale in both January and July, showing that they are dry all year round.

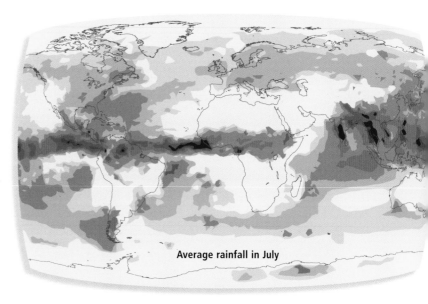

Average rainfall in July

Left: These rocks have been sculpted by the power of windblown sand. In many desert locations, wind, not water, is the most important force shaping the land.

The Gobi is a harsh place – dry, windswept and bitterly cold in winter – but the Takla Makan is much worse. In winter the temperature falls to about –24°C (–11°F), and the wind makes it feel even colder. In summer, though, the Takla Makan is hot, with temperatures around 30°C (86°F). It is a sandy desert, with great expanses of dunes that are constantly shifting between small, bare hills, where the rock has been swept clean of sand. Sandstorms are common and often last for days.

The Gobi and the Takla Makan are continental deserts: they're dry because they are thousands of kilometres from the ocean. Moist air from the sea sheds most of its water as rain on its journey inland, and then it has

Dust storms can be unpleasant and dangerous. Some animals, such as camels, close their nostrils and shield their eyes from the sand with long eyelashes. These oryx are taking cover beneath a tree.

to cross high mountains, where it loses the rest. By the time it reaches the Gobi and the Takla Makan the air is bone dry. The deserts are cold partly because they are high above sea level, but also because they are well to the north of the tropics.

By the sea

Continental deserts are dry because they are so far inland. So you might think that a desert could never exist right next to the coast. But you'd be wrong. There are deserts like that, and they include the driest deserts of all. The Namib Desert, for instance, which runs along the coast of south-west Africa, receives about 50 mm (2 in) of rain on average each year; London gets about the same in a month. And certain parts of the Namib are even drier. The Namib town of Swakopmund, for instance, has an annual rainfall of only 14 mm (0.6 in). The Namib is not baking, though – the daily temperature does not vary much, and is about 22°C (72°F) throughout the year.

The world's driest desert is the Atacama in South America, which stretches for about 965 km (600 miles) along the coast of Chile and southern Peru. There are places in the Atacama where it has rained no more than four times a century. Iquique, a town in north Chile, once went for four years with no rain, then a single shower fell in July of the fifth year. For people in Iquique, July is now the rainy season! At Arica, to the north of Iquique, the average annual rainfall is a minuscule 0.9 mm (0.03 in). It's hard to

Climographs

Each place in the world has its own pattern of weather. The typical pattern of weather that happens in one place during a year is called climate. We can sum up a place's climate on a climograph, such as the one shown here for St Louis in the USA. The letters along the bottom are the months of the year. The numbers on the left and the small bars show rainfall, and the numbers on the right and the curvy line show temperature. You can see at a glance that St Louis is hottest in July, but December is the driest month.

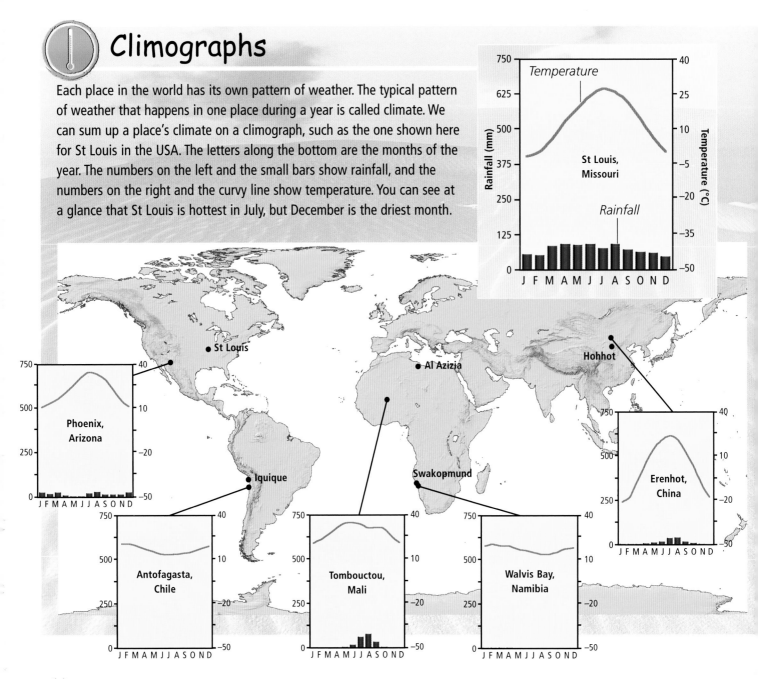

Young deserts

Compared to Earth's grand old age of 4.5 billion years, some of our planet's deserts are surprisingly young. The Great Basin in the USA, for instance, has been a desert for only about 12,000 years. About 15,000 years ago, forests covered the Great Basin, and mammoths, sabre-toothed cats and giant sloths roamed among the trees. When the ice age ended and the climate warmed, the desert began to form. The vast salt flats of the Great Basin, such as this one in Death Valley, are the parched remains of lakes that dried out.

Death Valley

California's Death Valley, near the edge of the Mojave Desert, is the hottest place in the USA and almost as hot as Al Azizia in Libya. The temperature in Death Valley can reach 57°C (135°F) in summer. In 1849, during the great California Gold Rush, a party of 30 settlers decided to take a shortcut to the gold fields. Their route took them through the valley, where twelve of them died from heat and thirst. That's how the valley got its name. Today it's a place for tourists.

imagine just how dry that is, but if you plan to visit you certainly won't need to pack an umbrella.

Fog but no rain

There's something very odd about the Namib and Atacama deserts. Despite the incredibly dry climate, the air in these deserts is very moist. Fog is common, and iron objects rust quickly. So how can these deserts exist when there is so much moisture in the air?

The cause of the peculiar climates is cold ocean currents near the coasts. The cold Benguela Current flows north along the coast of the Namib Desert, and the cold Peru (or Humboldt) Current flows north along the coast of the Atacama. The chilly water cools air travelling towards the land. Because the air gets cold, it stays low and doesn't rise

Flat-topped mountains like this are called mesas.

high enough to form clouds. That's why rain is so rare. It's also why these coastal deserts are relatively cool. At Lima, Peru, the average temperature is only 19°C (66°F) and doesn't change much through the year.

Air that has crossed the ocean is very moist because it picks up a lot of **water vapour**. When the moist air crosses a cold ocean current and cools down, its moisture condenses into tiny droplets, forming fog. It's a bit like exhaling on a cold day – the moisture in your breath condenses into mist as it hits the cold air. The cold ocean currents near the Atacama and Namib both produce sea fogs that roll into the desert regularly. Some plants and animals get nearly all their water by collecting the fog droplets.

Cold ocean currents tend to occur on the west coast of continents, so the Atacama and Namib are sometimes called west-coast deserts. Parts of the Sonoran Desert in Baja California and the part of the Sahara on the north-west coast of Africa are also west-coast deserts, with similar cold currents nearby.

Below: In this part of Patagonia, an ancient lava flow has been broken down by river action in an earlier, wetter time. Later, when Patagonia became a desert, the hills were eroded by wind.

Rain shadow

Patagonia is a cold desert region that covers most of Argentina. It is a different kind of desert from most others. It is neither in the subtropics, nor in the centre of a big continent thousands of miles from the sea, nor on a west coast. Why, then, is it so dry?

Patagonia lies in the 'rain shadow' of the Andes mountains. The wind in Patagonia comes mainly from the west, but before it reaches the desert it has to cross the high Andes. As the air rises over the mountains, it cools, causing moisture to condense and fall as rain, hail or snow. When the air reaches the far side of the mountains, it is very dry.

The wind occasionally blows from the east, across the nearby Atlantic Ocean. There, though, is yet another cold current, named the Falkland Current, for the air to cross. So air approaching from the east is chilled before it reaches the coast, like the air that reaches the Atacama and Namib deserts.

Patagonia is not the only desert in a rain shadow. North America's Great Basin owes its dry climate to the Sierra Nevada mountains, which cast a rain shadow over the region. However, only the valley bottoms in the Great Basin are true desert. The tops of many of the Great Basin's mountains catch just enough snow to support forests of conifer trees.

Atacama

The Atacama runs in a narrow strip between the Andes and the Pacific Ocean. This desert is so dry that nothing can live at its centre. Life is sustained by fog in the west and by water from the Andes in the east.

 ## Atacama facts

▲ The driest town in the world is Quillagua in the Atacama. In an average year it gets less than 0.5 mm (0.02 in) of rain.

▲ Many people in the Atacama see no rain at all for years at a time. Some people have never seen rain.

▲ Millions of pelicans, petrels, penguins and other seabirds, as well as sea lions and otters, use the desert coast to rest and breed. The emptiness of the desert protects them from land-based predators.

1. The Andes
To the east of the Atacama, the land rises towards the foothills of the Andes mountains. High peaks, including many active volcanoes, border the desert.

2. Guano
The ocean off the Atacama provides the richest fishing grounds on Earth. It supports countless seabirds, which nest on land. In the dry climate of the Atacama, the seabird droppings build up into deposits. People mine these deposits, called guano, to use as fertilizer.

3. Salar de Uyuni (Uyuni Salt Flat)
Up on the high, dry plateau of the Altiplano in Bolivia, this huge salt flat lies beyond the Atacama.

4. Cordillera de la Costa
This mountain range runs along the coast. In places, the mountains end in cliffs that plunge into the ocean and provide nest sites for millions of seabirds.

5. Chuquicamata copper mine
The largest open-cast copper mine on Earth.

6. Salar de Atacama (Atacama Salt Flat)
Most of the water has evaporated from this parched former lake bed, leaving salt deposits.

7. Valle de la Luna (Moon Valley)
The barren, gravel-strewn plains of this valley look like the surface of the Moon.

8. Peru (Humboldt) Current
This cold ocean current helps create the extreme desert conditions of the Atacama. It also creates fog – vital moisture for the Atacama's plants and animals.

9. Mount Ojos del Salado
At 6880 metres (22,573 ft), this is the highest active volcano in the world.

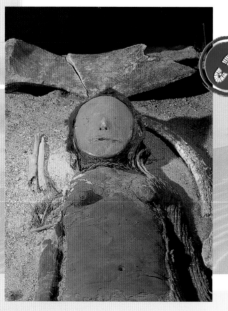

Morbid mummies

Amazingly, people have lived in the Atacama for at least 10,000 years. At first they lived on fish, shellfish and sea-lion meat, but later they irrigated land to grow corn and potatoes. As long ago as 5000 BC, the Chinchorro people began mummifying their dead. They first took the corpse apart and removed the flesh from the bones. Then they reassembled the skeleton and replaced the internal organs with bundles of reeds. They replaced the skin, and added patches of seal skin to cover any gaps. The mummy was finished with a decorative clay mask and a wig made from hair.

N

[1]

PERU

Juliaca

Arequipa

Pacific

Tacna

Arica

Ocean

[2]

Iquique

Atacama

Cordillera de la Costa

[4]

Quillagua

Tocopilla

Chuquicamata

[5]

Calama

Antofagasta

Peru Current

[8]

Desert

CHILE

[1]

Copiapó

Andes

The strange moonlike landscape of Valle de la Luna makes this valley a popular tourist site in the Atacama.

[7]

Potosí

[1]

Salar de Uyuni

[3]

BOLIVIA

Mount Aucanquilcha ▲

Ollagüe Volcano ▲

San Pedro Volcano ▲

Cordillera Domeyka

[6]

Mount Zapaleri ▲

Salar de Atacama

Valle de la Luna

[7]

Mount Rincón ▲

San Salvador de Jujuy

Salta

Llullaillaco ▲

Salar de Arizaro

Azufre Volcano ▲

ARGENTINA

[1]

[9]

Mount Ojos del Salado ▲

SOUTH AMERICA

[1]

0   100   miles
0   100   200 km

Desert plants

How can anything survive in a dry, scorching desert? Amazingly, there are many plants that can, from tiny 'living stones' the size of pebbles to giant cacti three times taller than a giraffe.

Plants need to be tough to survive in the desert. They have to deal with daytime temperatures that soar above 30°C (86°F) and night-time temperatures that plunge to freezing or below. Then they have to find water – and hang on to it. Finally, they have to protect themselves from hungry animals. To cope with these challenges, desert plants use all kinds of clever tricks.

Keeping cool

Plants elsewhere gather as much of the sun's energy as they possibly can, but desert plants are bathed in more sunlight than they can use. Lots of people wear light-coloured clothes in summer. That's because light colours reflect the sun's rays and so help keep you cool. Desert plants use the same method. Many of them are pale green or silvery grey, while the quiver tree of the Namib and Kalahari deserts of southern Africa grows branches that are covered in a chalky white powder.

The quiver tree of southern Africa stores water in the soft, spongy wood inside its trunk and branches. Local hunters find the branches easy to hollow out, and use them as quivers for their arrows.

Old-timers

Strangely enough, deserts are home to some of the longest-living plants in the world.

▲ Some bristlecone pines growing on the dry slopes of California's White Mountains are around 5000 years old. This means that they were already 500 years old when the ancient Egyptians built the great pyramids. The tallest of these trees are only 15 metres (50 ft) high – but it might have taken them 3000 years to reach this height.

▲ The creosote bush, which also grows in the deserts of California, sends out roots in all directions. From these roots grow a circle of clones (identical copies) of the original plant. Scientists calculate from the size of one circle that the original plant was alive nearly 12,000 years ago, when prehistoric people first started to grow crops.

▲ *Welwitschia* plants like the one below in the Namib Desert of southern Africa can live for up to 2000 years. Some started growing when the Roman Empire was at the peak of its power.

Getting a drink

Plants get most of the water they need through their roots. Because there is little water to be found in deserts, the plants that grow there need to send their roots very deep

The saguaro cactus, like many other cacti, has a ribbed surface. This allows it to expand like a concertina to absorb water.

to get as much water as possible. While deserts may be quite dry at the surface for most of the time, there is often water deep underground. To get at this water, some desert plants have a long, thick central root, called a taproot. The taproot of the mesquite tree, which grows in the American South-west, can pierce down 15 metres (50 ft) – the height of a five-storey building. The root of the camelthorn **acacia** tree of Africa can reach down twice as far.

Another way that a plant can collect scarce water is to spread its roots over a broad area, and this is exactly what many cacti do. They send out a wide net of hair-like roots in all directions, just below the surface. When it rains, the network of roots collects the water before it seeps deeper into the ground. The same roots can even absorb the dew that sometimes forms in deserts overnight.

Water from thin air

Other desert plants take in water through their leaves. One such plant is the bizarre *Welwitschia* of the Namib Desert in south-western Africa. The *Welwitschia* is a low-growing plant with long, tattered, strap-like leaves. These leaves can take in tiny droplets of water from the sea fogs that roll in from the Atlantic Ocean in the early morning – about the only regular source of water in the Namib.

The *Welwitschia* might look like a ragged mess, but it's a survivor. Many have lived for five to six hundred years in the Namib, which is one of the world's driest deserts, and some have lived much longer.

Storing water

Getting hold of water is only half the battle – desert plants also have to store it somewhere, because there might not be any more water around for a very long time.

Some kinds of plants are particularly good at storing water inside themselves. These plants are called **succulents**, which means juicy. The succulents include the cacti and agaves of the Americas and the euphorbias of Africa and Asia. Agaves have thick, fleshy, sword-shaped leaves spiking outwards from the centre of the plant. Euphorbias come in all shapes and sizes, from little herbs called spurges to spine-covered trees.

When it rains, cacti suck in huge amounts of water and swell up like balloons. The organ-pipe cactus, which grows three times taller than a man, can hold more than 380 litres (100 gallons) in its stem – enough to fill six bathtubs. This reservoir can see the cactus through four months of drought.

Plants don't have to be big to be good at surviving dry periods. For example, the wild tulips of the deserts of Central Asia live through most of the year as small underground bulbs. When the spring rains come, the bulbs quickly send up leaves and flowers. These die back at the start of the long summer, but the bulbs store enough food and water to last until

Like the saguaro cactus, the organ-pipe cactus is typical of the Sonoran Desert of Arizona and Mexico.

Homes in the desert

Although there are hardly any trees in the deserts of the American Southwest, the giant saguaro cacti are the next best thing as far as birds are concerned. The cacti have places for birds like the red-tailed hawk (left) to nest, and gila woodpeckers and elf owls nest in holes in the great stem. The camelthorn acacia tree of southern Africa also makes a home for many animals, including acacia rats and bushbabies (galagos).

Left: Many species of euphorbias live in African deserts. They are not cacti, but look just like cacti because they have thick, juicy stems that store water, and because they protect themselves with spines.

the next spring. The tulips that people grow in their gardens are all descended from these tough little desert survivors.

Preventing water loss

Once a plant has built up a good store of water, it needs to hang on to it. But no plant can avoid losing some water – it's part of the way they keep themselves alive.

All plants give off water vapour into the air. Most of the water vapour escapes through tiny pores (holes) in the leaves, which plants have to keep open to survive. The pores serve to take in **carbon dioxide**, a vital gas that they use to make food. So, to get carbon dioxide, plants have to lose a bit of water. Losing water can sometimes help them, though, because it makes their roots suck up

Right: Tulips, like this one growing in eastern Turkey, were taken to Belgium and Holland in the 16th century, starting the tulip-growing industry. They were so popular that some people made a fortune selling them.

more water from the ground, bringing up other useful chemicals with it. However, in the fiercely hot conditions of the desert, water evaporates from leaves too easily, and there's very little water in the ground to replace it. Most plants would quickly shrivel up and die, but desert plants have ways to stop this from happening.

Looking at a spiny cactus, you might think, 'That's a strange plant. It doesn't have any leaves'. Only spines emerge from its thick, fleshy stem. Cacti have lost their leaves and replaced them with small spikes that do not lose water. Instead of making food in leaves, they make food in the green stem, where there are far fewer pores.

In the Kara-Kum desert of Central Asia, the black saxaul tree uses an alternative method. For most of the year it has no leaves

Beckoning branches

Mormons named this desert plant the Joshua tree because they imagined its branches were the arms of the Hebrew leader Joshua beckoning them to the promised land. The Joshua tree is the largest type of yucca plant, and it lives in the Mojave Desert, where it has to cope with thin, rocky soil and extremely hot, dry weather. These conditions might seem inhospitable to us, but Joshua trees seem to like them – they live nowhere else.

Desert plants of North America

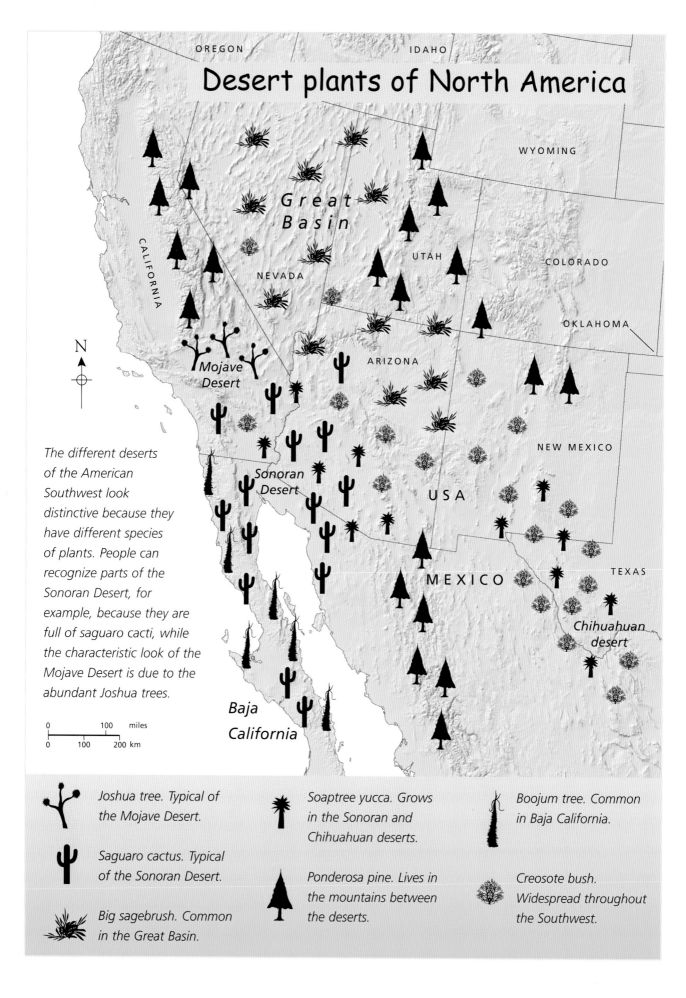

OREGON · IDAHO · WYOMING · CALIFORNIA · NEVADA · UTAH · COLORADO · OKLAHOMA · ARIZONA · NEW MEXICO · USA · MEXICO · TEXAS

Great Basin

Mojave Desert

Sonoran Desert

Baja California

Chihuahuan desert

The different deserts of the American Southwest look distinctive because they have different species of plants. People can recognize parts of the Sonoran Desert, for example, because they are full of saguaro cacti, while the characteristic look of the Mojave Desert is due to the abundant Joshua trees.

N

0   100   miles
0 100 200 km

Joshua tree. Typical of the Mojave Desert.

Saguaro cactus. Typical of the Sonoran Desert.

Big sagebrush. Common in the Great Basin.

Soaptree yucca. Grows in the Sonoran and Chihuahuan deserts.

Ponderosa pine. Lives in the mountains between the deserts.

Boojum tree. Common in Baja California.

Creosote bush. Widespread throughout the Southwest.

and makes food instead in its whitish-green twigs and branches. Once the tree has flowered, borne fruit and spread its seeds, it often sheds some of its branches to cut down evaporation even more.

Cacti, like the other succulent plants, only open their pores to take in carbon dioxide at night, when it's a lot cooler. At these low temperatures, very little water can evaporate.

Tubby plants

Many cacti have a shape that helps reduce water loss. You might think that all cacti are the tall, thin giants you see in cowboy movies, but most of them are small and squat and round. Spherical (round) shapes have a small surface area compared to their size. Since it's from the surface of plants that water evaporates, spherical cacti have the smallest possible surface area from which they can lose water. At the same time, they contain the greatest space for water storage.

Desert grasses also tend to have shapes that help them cut down on water loss. For example, esparto grass, which grows on the northern edge of the Sahara, has rolled-up leaves. Most of its pores are on the inside surface of the rolled leaf, so rolling shades its pores from the sun. In the semi-desert areas of south-west Asia, the spear grasses lay their leaves out flat when it rains, but roll them up when it gets hot and dry again.

Desert plants sometimes use chemicals as well as shape to stop them from losing water. Euphorbias have stems filled with a white, sticky, poisonous liquid that does not evaporate easily. Many desert plants ooze poisonous chemicals into the ground around them. This stops other plants from growing nearby and tapping into their water supplies. Other desert plants send out a dense mat of roots that stops other young plants from growing nearby. This is why plants in deserts are often spaced very regularly.

Desert feasts

In the deserts of the USA and Mexico, people eat some types of agaves. The leaves of agaves are tough, sword-shaped and spiky, but the stem and flowers of some types are delicious roasted, boiled or scrambled with eggs. In southern Africa, the local people have found all sorts of plant food in the Kalahari Desert. They get starch (a source of sugar) from some corms and tubers (swollen roots), and protein from foods such as mongongo nuts and tsin beans. The fruits of the marula tree (related to the mango) and the bottle-shaped baobab tree are both full of vitamin C. The Kalahari is also home to the wild watermelon (below), which quenches the thirst of both people and animals.

Self-defence

In the deserts of the American Southwest, the chemicals in the sagebrush not only poison the ground around it but also give the plant a revolting taste. Being poisonous is one sure way that a plant can protect itself from being eaten.

Another well-known example of chemical defence is the creosote bush. Its leaves contain a poisonous oil that smells

One desert plant makes itself even more difficult to eat by hiding underground. This is the window plant of the Namib Desert, which buries its plump, upright leaves under the surface. Only the tips of the leaves appear above the surface. These tips – the 'windows' – are made of a see-through material that lets sunlight reach the rest of the leaves below ground. Burying its leaves underground also helps the window plant cut down on water loss.

The next best thing to staying completely out of sight is to use a disguise. The living stones of the Namib Desert look just like pebbles. Only when you peer at them very closely can you see that the round stone is made up of two mottled, fleshy lumps that are in fact leaves. From a distance, people can recognize a living stone as a plant only when it flowers – but the flowers, although wonderfully bright and colourful to attract insects, last only for a couple of days.

The stumpy, rounded shape of these living stones makes them look like small pebbles – useful for camouflage, but also good for preventing water loss.

like creosote, the foul-smelling chemical that people use to preserve timber. Only the creosote bush grasshopper can stand the disgusting taste.

Desert plants also have more visible defences. Cacti, agaves and desert euphorbias are all armed with sharp spines. Some cacti, such as the cholla of American deserts, also have barbed bristles, while a large variety of desert trees and shrubs, such as acacias, are covered in vicious thorns. The milkweed plant of south-west Asia has long ribs between its leaves. When the ribs die they become hard and sharp, forming a kind of spiky cage around the flowers. Milkweed also grows very close to the ground, which makes it more difficult for animals to eat.

 # Cactus facts

▲ There are more than 1600 species of cactus. They live on the American continents, all the way from Canada to Argentina.

▲ The smallest cactus is about 1 cm (0.5 inches) across. The largest is the saguaro cactus, which can grow as tall as 18 metres (60 ft).

▲ Large cacti can take in 800 litres (210 gallons) of water at one time when it rains.

▲ A saguaro cactus 6 metres (20 ft) tall can hold more than a tonne of water in its stem.

▲ Many wild cacti are protected by law. People who steal a saguaro cactus in parts of the USA can be given a heavy fine or even a jail sentence.

Heavy rainstorms often soak the North American deserts in spring. Cacti and other plants burst into flower after the rain, and insects emerge to feed on the nectar.

The blooming desert

We don't normally think of deserts as colourful places, but in the Sonoran Desert in Arizona and Mexico, millions of flowers sometimes appear together in spring, after winter rainstorms. They are 'ephemerals' – plants whose life cycle lasts a matter of days. For most of the time only their seeds are present, lying dormant (inactive) in the soil. After heavy rain, they sprout, burst into flower and quickly produce more seeds before the ground dries out. Then they shrivel up and die. Desert ephemerals include poppies, daisies and members of the pea family. The seeds can survive years waiting for rain, but they take as little as two hours to produce leaves once they get soaked.

Kalahari and Namib

The Kalahari stretches across Botswana, while the red sands of the Namib run down the coast of Namibia into South Africa. The Kalahari is not the driest of deserts, but the Namib has so little water that its plants and animals must rely on fog.

 ## Fact file

▲ The Skeleton Coast in the Namib Desert is one of the world's driest places. Some people think it is named for the remains of shipwrecked sailors who died there before finding water.

▲ The Okavango River is overwhelmed by the sandy dryness of the Kalahari and peters out into a swampy wetland, the Okavango Delta.

▲ On the Namib coast, jackass penguins dig nesting burrows in the guano (hardened deposits of bird droppings) from millions of other seabirds.

▲ The name Kalahari comes from a word in the Tswana language meaning 'the great thirst'.

 ## Collecting fog

There is hardly any rain in the Namib, but there is a cold-water current in the nearby Atlantic Ocean. The cold water creates fog, which rolls in from the ocean on most mornings. Any moisture available to plants and animals comes in the form of this fog. Some Namib beetles have a cunning way of getting a drink. In the early morning, the beetles stand on the sand with their back ends raised in the air and catch fog droplets on their bodies. The tiny drops of water then join and trickle down towards the beetles' mouths.

A fog bank shows the immense height of the sand dunes on the Namib coast, some of which rise to 300 metres (1000 ft).

1. Skeleton Coast
This stretch of desolate, extremely arid coast is now a national park.

2. Walvis Bay
Millions of Cape fur seals and seabirds breed here on the desert coast. They feed in the rich fishing grounds offshore.

3. Sossusvlei
One of many pans: shallow depressions in the land that flood after heavy rains. Nearby, sand dunes 300 metres (1000 ft) tall are called 'sand mountains'.

4. Diamond mines
Deposits of diamonds lie under the sands of the Namib. Namibia's most important mine is at the mouth of the Orange River.

5. Etosha Pan
Another large, shallow depression that is usually composed of dry salt flats but when flooded attracts hordes of animals.

6. Dry rivers
The Kalahari has virtually no surface water. Its rivers have dry beds most of the time and flow only in unusually wet months.

7. Okavango Delta
The water here attracts a world-famous spectacular array of wildlife, including elephants, wildebeest, zebras and lions.

8. CKGR
The Central Kalahari Game Reserve (CKGR) protects the hunting and gathering lifestyle of the San people.

9. Makgadikgadi salt pans
This series of salt pans fills with water when the Okavango Delta overflows during wet weather.

Desert animals

We often think of deserts as empty places, where no animals live. In fact, a great variety of animals are at home in deserts, from tiny insects to large mammals like antelopes and camels. There are even elephants living in deserts.

All land animals depend on plants for food. Either they eat plants themselves, or they eat other animals that feed on plants.

In the driest deserts there are hardly any plants, so plant-eating animals can survive only by eating seeds or other bits of plants blown into the desert by the wind. Such food is enough only for very small animals, like insects. Spiders, snakes and lizards eat the insects, and they, in turn, are eaten by larger animals, such as birds of prey.

Wetter deserts have a wider range of plants, including grasses, cacti, shrubs or even scattered trees. Deserts that are rich in plant life provide enough food for larger animals, such as rabbits, antelopes, camels and – in Australia – kangaroos. In Africa, herds of antelope travel huge distances to find enough plants to keep them alive, and **predators** such as lions and leopards often follow them into the desert in the hope of an easy meal. Other desert hunters include

There is hardly anything to eat on the dunes of the Namib Desert in southern Africa. Oryx, a kind of antelope, survive there by drinking at the water holes and eating the sparse plants on the plains.

coyotes and foxes in the deserts of North America, and pumas in the cold Patagonian desert of South America.

Most desert animals can't afford to be too fussy about what they eat, but some have very particular requirements. The yucca moth, for example, depends entirely on yucca plants for its survival – and yucca plants depend just as much on the moth.

Yuccas are plants with a rosette of long, sharp-tipped leaves surrounding a flower stalk in the middle. The female yucca moth lays her eggs in the middle of a yucca flower, and the caterpillars that hatch feed on a few of the developing seeds inside the flower. To make sure the flower will make seeds, the moth first collects a ball of pollen from a different yucca flower, and then rubs this on her chosen flower after laying the eggs. No other insect can pollinate the yucca flower, and no other flower provides a suitable home for the caterpillars – so yuccas and yucca moths depend on each other to survive.

Another specialist feeder is the gerenuk, a long-necked gazelle that lives in the deserts of Somalia in east Africa (*gerenuk* means 'giraffe-necked' in the Somali language). The gerenuk feeds on the leaves of thorny bushes. By standing on its hind legs and stretching its long neck, it can reach much higher leaves than other animals can.

The remarkable spadefoot toad

You wouldn't think deserts were a good place for toads to live. Most toads, like other amphibians, must keep themselves moist. But certain amphibians manage to survive in very dry conditions. Some spadefoot toads live in the deserts of western North America. They lay their eggs in the small pools that appear after rainfall. The tadpoles that hatch from these eggs can turn into toads in as little as two weeks – much quicker than most other tadpoles. This is because tadpoles can't live out of water, so they need to develop quickly before the pool dries up.

Spadefoots get their name from the spade-like growth on their hind feet. This helps them burrow down into the soil where they escape the dry heat of the desert. They only ever come out of the soil at night, during a short time in spring and early summer when they frantically breed. They spend the rest of their time buried alive. They might not emerge for eleven months of each year.

Many types of scorpions, such as this bark scorpion of California, have made deserts their own. In some places there is a greater total weight of scorpions than any other animals except ants and termites.

Finding water

Like a number of other desert animals, the gerenuk never has to drink – it gets all the water it needs from the leaves it eats. In fact, all animals can make water inside their bodies by a chemical reaction. This water comes from the chemical process that releases energy from food. Some desert rodents get nearly all their water this way.

Other desert animals can go without drinking for a long time. Camels can survive for a week without drinking when they are working, and for several months when they're not. When they do drink, they can take in over 100 litres (26 gallons) – more than a bathtub-full – in one session. People often think that camels store water in their humps, but the humps are full of fatty tissue. Camels use this as a sort of emergency food supply, and it can be broken down inside the camel's body to release water.

Finding water is not easy in the desert. Large desert animals like antelopes travel long distances to get to water holes, where they can drink. Some antelopes, as well as wild horses and asses, are good at breaking up the dry ground with their hooves to get at

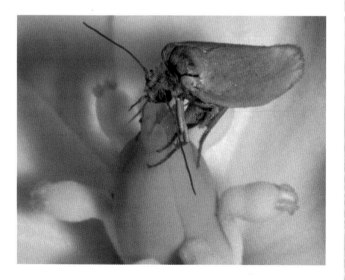

The yucca moth has a very close partnership with yucca plants. The moth helps the plant reproduce, while the plant provides a meal for the moth's caterpillars.

 ## Desert makers

Animals can help make deserts. During the time of the ancient Romans, parts of North Africa were much greener than today, and the Romans even grew wheat in the region. After the fall of the Roman Empire, the complicated irrigation systems that watered the crops fell into ruin. Rather than growing wheat, people took to raising sheep and goats. If there are too many sheep and goats in an area, the animals strip the vegetation – grass, shrubs, trees, everything. They also eat any new shoots that appear, so there is no chance for plants to recover. This process, called overgrazing, can turn fertile land into a desert. In North Africa today you can still see the ruins of magnificent Roman towns, surrounded by desert.

small amounts of water under the surface. The thorny devil, a spiky lizard from Australia, has scales on its body that can soak up water from damp sand.

It's important for desert animals not to lose water. Animals lose water when they urinate, but they have to urinate to get rid of waste products in the body. This process is called **excretion**. To reduce water loss, camels and other desert animals have very concentrated urine; in other words, their urine contains only a small amount of water, which makes it particularly dark and smelly. Some desert reptiles excrete solid crystals instead of liquid urine. Other reptiles get rid of certain waste products, such as salts, through glands on the sides of their snouts.

Wasting nothing

Animals also lose water in their droppings, so most desert animals have very dry droppings. Camel dung is incredibly dry and solid – for thousands of years desert people have used it as a fuel instead of firewood, which is hard to find in the desert. North American kangaroo rats make sure they don't waste any water in their droppings by eating them.

Another way animals lose water is by sweating. Sweating is a way of keeping cool, but camels can stand being warmer than most other mammals before they need to start sweating. They have fewer sweat glands than other animals, and their thick coat keeps the scorching sunlight off their skin, which stops them from getting too hot.

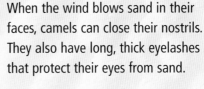 # One hump or two?

There are two kinds of camels. The Arabian camel (also called a dromedary, below) has one hump. It lives in North Africa and south-west Asia. It is now a domestic animal, although some of the camels introduced to Australia in the 19th century have become wild. The other kind of camel is the two-humped Bactrian camel, which lives in Central Asia. Most Bactrian camels are also domesticated (bred), but there are still a few wild herds in remote parts of Mongolia and western China. Camels are sometimes called ships of the desert because they are so good at carrying goods and people across seas of sand. They can keep going for a long time without food or water, and have many other ways of dealing with life in the desert. For example, camels have a web of skin joining the two toes on each foot. This web spreads out as they walk, keeping the foot from sinking into soft sand. It's a bit like wearing snowshoes. When the wind blows sand in their faces, camels can close their nostrils. They also have long, thick eyelashes that protect their eyes from sand.

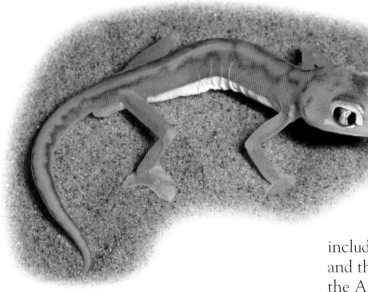

Above: Sand in desert dunes is so loose that animals can swim through it. Some small geckos even have webbed feet, like a frog's feet, to help them swim.

Surviving heat and cold

Many deserts are very hot during the day, but at night the temperature can plummet to freezing. To avoid the heat of the day, small desert animals often shelter under rocks or dig burrows. Some animals only come out at night, when it's cooler. Night-time hunters include the fennec (a fox of North Africa) and the western diamondback rattlesnake of the American Southwest. The western diamondback has little pits beneath its eyes that can detect infrared radiation (heat). This helps it 'see' its prey – usually warm-blooded rodents – in the dark.

Sometimes it gets too cold to go out at night. Animals like the kangaroo rat of North America and the mouse-like jerboa of Asia and North Africa come out of their shelters mainly at dawn and dusk, when the temperature is most comfortable.

Ears that radiate

Jerboas, which are also called desert rats, have very long hind legs that enable them to hop along quickly. They also have big ears. Other desert mammals, like the fennec and the similar kit fox of the American South-west, have big ears, too. A big, flat ear is like a radiator. There is very little volume and a lot of surface area to give off (radiate) heat. So big ears help lose heat from the animal's body and keep the animal cool.

Most birds have a higher body temperature than mammals. Nevertheless, the intense desert sun would cause them to overheat unless they had some method of cooling off.

This round-tailed ground squirrel lives in the American deserts. It gets all the water it needs from its food, but it needs food rich in water, such as this cactus flower.

Not all oryx make it in the harsh
environment of the Namib Desert.
The remains of this one might
have been scavenged by jackals
and hyenas, which range widely
across the dunes.

Desert animals of Asia

The deserts of central Asia are barren. The sparse rains support few plants, so the food supply for animals is meagre. Plant-eating mammals such as the wild ass, Bactrian camel and Mongolian gazelle travel widely to find enough grazing. Even outside the migrating season, gazelles cover more than 20 km (12 miles) per day in their endless search for food.

Meat eaters in the desert must make the most of each rare opportunity to feed. So while the corsac fox and the steppe eagle hunt desert rodents, they also survive by scavenging carcasses whenever they can.

The houbara bustard is also a flexible feeder and has a wide taste in food. It collects seeds and shoots but also preys on locusts, beetles and lizards when it finds them.

Asiatic wild ass

Bactrian camel

Steppe eagle

Mongolian gazelle

Houbara bustard

Corsac fox

Many desert birds have a way of fanning themselves to keep cool: they flutter a patch of skin on their throats.

Sunbathing reptiles

Birds and mammals are sometimes called **warm-blooded** because their bodies are always at the same warm temperature. They use a lot of energy in keeping their bodies at the right temperature, and all this energy comes from their food. In fact, they use about 90 per cent of the food they eat to keep their body temperature steady.

Cold-blooded animals, such as snakes and lizards, don't need to keep their bodies at a steady temperature. They can spend most of their time cold and inactive, using very little energy. Because of this, reptiles can get by on a tenth of the food that mammals and birds need. This gives snakes and lizards an advantage in deserts, where food is scarce.

Cold-blooded isn't a very good description, because a reptile's body temperature changes with that of its surroundings. Its body is colder than a mammal's at night, but at midday in the desert it might be warmer.

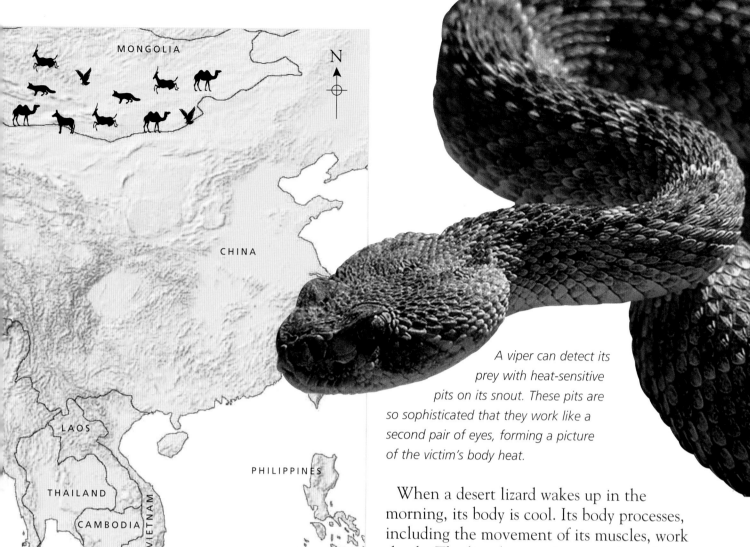

A viper can detect its prey with heat-sensitive pits on its snout. These pits are so sophisticated that they work like a second pair of eyes, forming a picture of the victim's body heat.

When a desert lizard wakes up in the morning, its body is cool. Its body processes, including the movement of its muscles, work slowly. The lizard can only move sluggishly, but once it has crawled from its shelter and into the sun, it begins to warm up. Moving slowly is one disadvantage of being cold-blooded, especially if a warm-blooded predator is on the prowl. When the lizard is warm, its muscles work quickly enough for it to scuttle about looking for food, or escape from birds of prey. As the air gets hotter, desert lizards often climb to the higher branches of a bush, where there is more breeze to cool them. By midday, when the sun is at its hottest, the lizard might look for shade under a rock.

Being cold-blooded has other advantages in the desert. Animals lose water as they breathe, but cold-blooded animals only need

The Arabian jerboa is one of the many desert rodents that scrape out a living scurrying beneath the thin desert soil by day, coming out to steal seeds at night.

to breathe very, very slowly when they are resting. As a result, reptiles lose much less water than birds or mammals. And while mammals have to sweat to cool themselves in hot weather, cold-blooded animals simply let their bodies heat up. This allows reptiles to survive on much less water than mammals or birds, making them expert desert dwellers.

Staying out of the heat

Some desert animals, like spiders and scorpions, avoid the problems of heat and lack of water by becoming **dormant**. When an animal is dormant, it stays completely inactive – sometimes for weeks or months on end. It neither eats nor moves, and appears so lifeless that it seems to be dead. Dormant animals wake up only when there is a chance of eating something, or of mating. In the Sahara, desert snails can remain dormant for years until brought back to life by rain. In Australia, various kinds of tiny shrimps lie dormant in the desert. The wind blows their eggs until they settle in a crevice or a hollow in rock, and the eggs stay there until it rains. When the hollow fills up with water, the eggs hatch. Such shrimps have even been found in hollows high up on the sun-baked sides of Uluru (Ayers Rock), the famous giant rock in the middle of the Australian desert. Some birds search for food in the desert, but they build their nests in more comfortable places beyond the

The Australian desert pool where these shield shrimps live is drying up. But when it forms again with the next rains, the shrimps' eggs are ready to hatch and grow, before any other pond creatures arrive in the pool.

edge of the desert, such as forests, mountains or grasslands. This is no problem for birds like eagles and vultures, which can fly great distances with little effort. These birds also have incredibly sharp vision and can spot an animal on the ground from a long way off. By roaming vast areas, such birds can find just enough food for themselves and their distant chicks back at the nest.

The strange duckbill of the shovelnosed lizard helps it burrow in the loose sand of the Namib Desert. It can quickly plunge in to extract prey such as this fly.

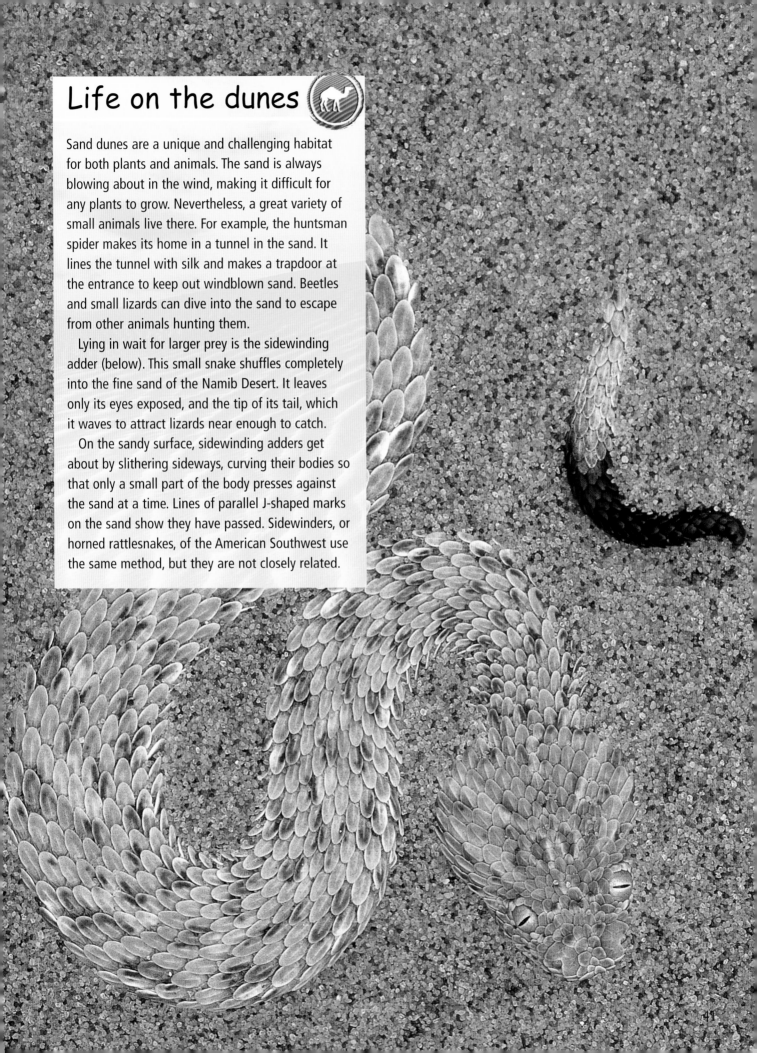

Life on the dunes

Sand dunes are a unique and challenging habitat for both plants and animals. The sand is always blowing about in the wind, making it difficult for any plants to grow. Nevertheless, a great variety of small animals live there. For example, the huntsman spider makes its home in a tunnel in the sand. It lines the tunnel with silk and makes a trapdoor at the entrance to keep out windblown sand. Beetles and small lizards can dive into the sand to escape from other animals hunting them.

Lying in wait for larger prey is the sidewinding adder (below). This small snake shuffles completely into the fine sand of the Namib Desert. It leaves only its eyes exposed, and the tip of its tail, which it waves to attract lizards near enough to catch.

On the sandy surface, sidewinding adders get about by slithering sideways, curving their bodies so that only a small part of the body presses against the sand at a time. Lines of parallel J-shaped marks on the sand show they have passed. Sidewinders, or horned rattlesnakes, of the American Southwest use the same method, but they are not closely related.

Sahara

The Sahara stretches across North Africa, from the Atlantic Ocean to the Red Sea. It is the largest desert and covers one-twelfth of Earth's land surface.

 ## Desert mammals

Mammals in the Sahara avoid the scorching heat by staying underground during the day. The fennec, a kind of fox, hides out in its burrows in large family groups. Nevertheless, to survive in the Sahara, it must have the ability to go without a drink for long periods. At night the fennec comes out to hunt small rodents, lizards and insects such as locusts. Its densely furred feet allow it to run fast on loose sand, and it can keep cool by losing body heat through its huge ears.

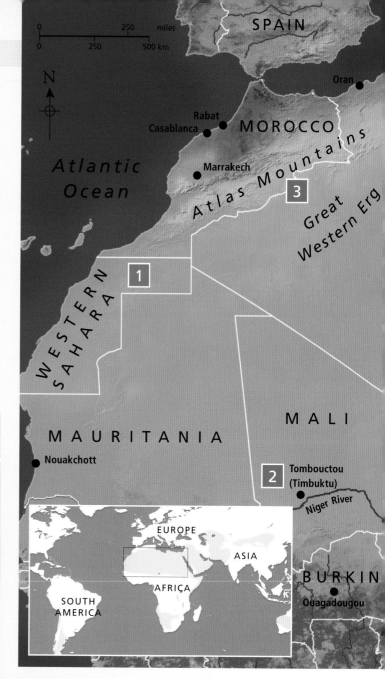

 ## Sahara facts

▲ The Sahara covers parts of eleven countries: Morocco, Algeria, Tunisia, Libya, Egypt, Western Sahara, Mauritania, Mali, Niger, Chad and Sudan.

▲ The desert ends gradually in the south as it blends with the belt of semi-desert called the Sahel.

▲ Few people live in the Sahara. On average there is less than one person per square kilometre (0.4 square miles) – the same as Alaska.

Together with the seasonal streams that fill valleys called wadis, oases such as this one are important life-supporting features of the Sahara.

1. Disputed territory
Both Morocco and Mauritania have made claims for the region called Western Sahara. The area used to be administered by Spain.

2. Tombouctou (Timbuktu)
For centuries this city has been both a trading post for merchants crossing the Sahara and a centre of Islamic culture and learning.

3. Atlas Mountains
Stretching across northern Algeria and Morocco, these mountains mark the northwestern border of the Sahara.

4. The Great Ergs, or Sand Seas
The Sahara has varied terrain, but seas of sand dunes such as the Great Ergs cover a quarter of its area.

5. Oil fields
The Sahara's richest oil fields occur in southern Algeria and eastern Libya. Half of Africa's known oil reserves are in Libya.

6. Chott al Jerid
A vast, flat salt lake. The lake sometimes holds water in winter, but it dries out in summer.

7. Chad Basin
A huge wetland that is only a fraction of its former size. Due to climate change, arid lands and salt pans now cover much of the area once covered by the waters of Lake Chad.

8. Tibesti Mountains
At 3415 metres (11,204 ft), Mount Koussi in the Tibesti Mountains is the highest point of land in the Sahara.

9. Al Khufra Oasis
This group of five oases covers an area the size of Israel.

10. Lake Nasser
An artificial reservoir created in 1971 by the completion of the Aswan High Dam. Its waters irrigate land to the north.

People and the desert

Imagine living in a desert – and surviving. You would have to protect yourself against extreme temperatures. You would have to find food and water when both are in short supply. Knowing the way to the nearest water hole could be a matter of life or death.

This satellite image of electric lights on Earth at night reveals where people are most concentrated. Compare it with the map on pages 6–7, and you'll notice that many of the darkest areas are deserts. However, the deserts in the USA and Saudi Arabia contain lots of light. These countries have enough resources to build cities in the desert.

From time to time, you would also have to cope with natural events such as sandstorms and flash floods. Life can be very hard in the desert, and to survive you have to be very resourceful.

Despite such difficulties, people have lived in the desert for thousands of years. Some have been **nomadic**, travelling from place to place in search of the scarce resources available. Others have settled at **oases**, using these rare desert springs to grow crops or to water cattle. Some have even founded bustling cities, which thrived on passing trade.

Like desert plants and animals, desert people have learned to adapt to their harsh environment. Physically, people are not well suited to the desert. Like other mammals, we are warm-blooded, which makes coping with very high or low temperatures difficult. Being warm-blooded also means we need a steady supply of food and water. Over thousands of years, desert people have developed unique lifestyles that meet these challenges. They have gathered

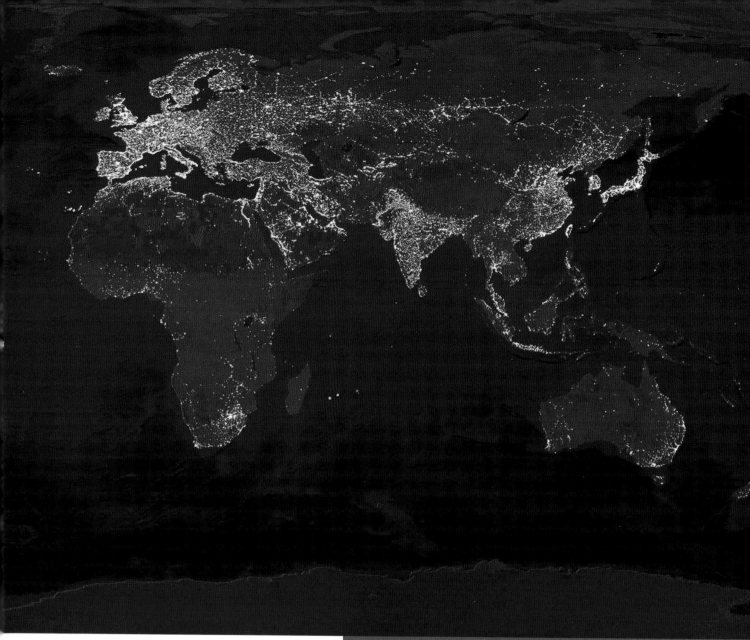

 # What to wear in the desert

You might think that the best way to dress in the desert would be to wear as little as possible. Certainly, a few desert peoples, such as the San of southern Africa and the Aborigines of Australia, wore few or no clothes in the past. However, most desert dwellers wear a lot of loose-fitting clothes. These help keep the body cool by shading the skin from the scorching sun. In the Sahara (right), a man might wear long trousers, a long, flowing upper garment and a turban wrapped around his head.

in the most unlikely places. An important part of the diet of the desert-dwelling Aborigines of Australia is still the witchety grub. Women and children dig up the roots of acacia bushes and cut them up to find the grubs. They eat the grubs raw or cooked in ashes. The grubs are so rich in fat, vitamins and protein that just ten of them provide enough food for a day.

Many desert nomads were animal herders, and some people still live this way today. Such people usually herd sturdy animals, like goats and camels, which cope well with the dry climate. The animals provide leather for sandals and tents, as well as milk and, less often, meat. During the driest months, nomadic herders linger in more **fertile** lands close to towns and cities, but during the rainy season they move farther into the desert.

A Bedouin welcome

Some of the best-known desert herders are the Bedouin of the Arabian, Syrian and North African deserts. The word *bedouin* comes from an Arabic word meaning 'desert dweller', and it includes many different peoples of the region. Like other nomads, the Bedouin have to carry their possessions with them, including their shelter – a light and portable tent made of goat skin or woven camel hair. The tent provides not only shade during the day but warmth at night. Bedouin tents can be very elaborate. They are often divided into two sections by a woven curtain. One section is reserved for men and for male visitors; the other is where women prepare meals and receive female guests. Bedouins treat guests with great honour, and ply them with lots of fresh, spice-flavoured coffee or mint tea.

an in-depth knowledge of **arid** (dry) landscapes and ecology, and have learned to respect the power of the desert.

Water, food and shelter

In the past, many desert people were nomads. A nomad is a person who travels frequently in search of food or water. Because there is so little water in the desert, nomads often had to travel far from one water hole or oasis to another, and they often carried a supply of water with them. The San people of the Kalahari Desert in Africa sometimes use a very unusual container to hold their water – a hollow ostrich egg. The shell of an ostrich egg is very strong and large, making a perfect flask for a long day of hunting.

The difficulty of desert life meant that everyone was kept busy. In some societies, the men went hunting while the women and children gathered fruits, roots and other foods. Desert nomads found food and water

The nutritious, nutty-flavoured witchety grub is the young form of a moth, so it is really a kind of caterpillar. It lives in the roots of desert acacia trees in Australia.

Finding the way

To a stranger's eyes, a desert may look featureless and monotonous. To the eyes of a nomad, however, it is full of information – a dry riverbed, a distinctive baobab tree or an odd-shaped rock can all help desert people find their way. In very early times, desert nomads probably made simple maps, drawn on bark or leather, that told them where to find good water or where dangers lurked. Today, Aborigines still avoid getting lost by following routes that people have used for centuries. The routes pass water holes, hunting grounds and natural landmarks. Walkers memorize the way by learning a map chant – a kind of verbal map that is passed from generation to generation.

Until the 20th century, there were few paved roads or railways in the world's deserts, and many desert people travelled on foot. This could be hard work, especially on rocky ground or hot, slippery sand. To protect their feet against heat and rough surfaces, some desert people wore leather sandals or shoes. However, many people, including Bedouin and Aborigines, went barefoot.

From early times, the desert people of Asia used camels both to ride on and to carry goods and possessions. Camels are very tough

 # Desert civilization in the south-west

The deserts of the south-west USA and Mexico were home to people centuries before contact with Europeans. The traces of the culture of some of these people are still visible today. The Sinagua, or Western Anasazi, for example, built multi-storey cliff dwellings and developed a kind of dry farming using the sparse water available. They also used a system of irrigation to support farming in the desert. The Anasazi civilization declined in the 13th century, but the people left their buildings, such as Montezuma's Castle in Arizona (right).

The people that met the invaders from Europe and the USA in the 19th century did not live in the same way as the Sinagua. They had a range of different lifestyles, from hunting and gathering to settled agriculture.

animals and can travel for days without drinking. They also provide milk, wool and meat. Nothing is wasted. Bedouins use camel dung for fuel, and camel urine for shampoo.

Camels, trains and automobiles

Camels played an especially important role in **caravans**. These were parties of traders or pilgrims who travelled together across the desert for safety, much like the wagon trains of the American pioneers. The largest caravans included thousands of camels. In 1908, for example, a caravan carrying salt across the Sahara numbered 20,000 camels. Caravans often moved by night to avoid walking in the daytime heat.

European explorers in Australia brought camels to the continent to help them on their long, dangerous treks across the

Some desert nomads rely on their animals for almost everything. These nomads in Iran use animal skins as water carriers, and weave goat hair into a lightweight fabric to make their tents.

outback, the interior region of Australia. Robert Burke (1820/21–1861) and William Wills (1834–1861) were the first white men to cross Australia south to north, in 1861. They used 24 camels to carry their equipment, which included 20 camp beds, 80 pairs of shoes and 30 hats. But even the camels could not survive the gruelling journey. By the time Burke and Wills died of starvation and exhaustion on the return trek, all of their camels were dead, too.

The efforts of explorers like Burke and Wills helped open up the Australian outback to European settlers. In south Australia, settlers hired 'cameleers' (camel drivers) from Afghanistan. The cameleers carried supplies, passengers and post on the long trip between Adelaide, on the south coast, and the desert settlement of Alice Springs in the centre of Australia. Later, when a railway was built between the two towns, it was named Ghan in honour of the Afghan cameleers.

Exploring the Arabian Desert

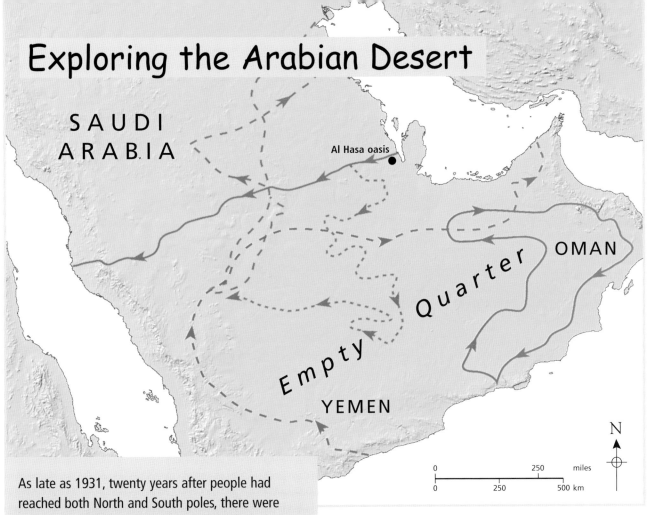

SAUDI ARABIA

Al Hasa oasis

Empty Quarter

OMAN

YEMEN

N

| 0 | | 250 | miles |
| 0 | 250 | 500 km | |

As late as 1931, twenty years after people had reached both North and South poles, there were still regions of the Arabian Desert where no European had set foot. The explorer Harry St. John Philby was already an experienced desert traveller when he finally traversed the Empty Quarter in 1932. European travellers such as Wilfred Thesiger later reported that the Empty Quarter is not quite as devoid of human life as once thought. Thesiger met people that lived off the land even there.

──────── Philby (1917)

─ ─ ─ ─ Philby (1918)

· · · · · · Philby (1932)

──────── Thesiger (1946–1947)

─ ─ ─ ─ Thesiger (1947–1948)

Today, even the world's most remote deserts are crossed by roads, tracks and the occasional railway. Many desert peoples have abandoned camels for four-wheel-drive cars. Even so, driving in the desert can be very dangerous. Wise motorists carry plenty of water in case of emergencies. On desert roads in Saudi Arabia, there are solar-powered satellite telephones beside the highways, in case an automobile breaks down.

Settling the desert

Nomads are not the only people to have eked out a living in the desert. Since ancient times, desert people have also built permanent settlements. Many villages grew up in shady oases, where there was a reliable supply of water. Often the villagers dug deep wells to reach water trapped in layers of rock below ground. The water usually did not have to be pumped out because it sprang up naturally under its own pressure.

One of the oldest oasis settlements is the Egyptian village of Siwa, deep in the Libyan Desert. In ancient times it was the site of a temple to the Egyptian god Amon. Life at Siwa has changed very little over many centuries. The inhabitants are Berbers, an ancient people who have lived in North

Islands in the desert

In some deserts, such as the Sahara of North Africa, there are a few places where there is always water. Such a place is called an oasis. You find oases where water from deep underground bubbles up to the surface, forming a spring. Palm trees and other plants that cannot normally survive in the desert grow around the water.

Oases are important resting places for people and camels travelling across the desert. They are also important for migrating birds, which stop at oases to drink and feed on the fruits of the trees. Some oases, such as this one in Morocco, support a lush growth of date palms and other important crops. Oases now draw tourists as well as desert people. In some areas, people are discovering that more money can be made if the oasis water is used for golf courses instead of date palms.

Africa for thousands of years. At Siwa, they live in mud-brick houses and make their living from the thousands of palm and olive trees that flourish in the lush oasis.

Oases can be very large, supporting a whole region of towns and villages. On the northern edge of the Empty Quarter in the southern Arabian Peninsula is the Al Hasa oasis, which covers some 12,000 hectares – about the size of Glasgow. Its 3 million palm trees are watered by over sixty springs. After the discovery of oil fields in the surrounding region in the 1930s, Al Hasa became even more prosperous. Today, Al Hasa is connected to the Saudi capital, Riyadh, by a paved highway as well as a railway.

The discovery of oil and other minerals beneath some desert regions has led to further settlement of the desert. Riyadh itself was once a small, walled desert town. In the years following the discovery of oil in Saudi Arabia in 1938, the town boomed. The oil-rich Saudi kings and businessmen built luxurious palaces, mosques, hotels and suburbs, and today the capital has a population of more than 1.3 million people.

Exploiting the desert

Once deserts were considered good-for-nothing wildernesses. Today, many of the world's deserts – including the Sahara, the Kara-Kum and the Arabian deserts – are known to lie over vast deposits of oil and gas. Oil pipelines crisscross these deserts, carrying oil and gas to refineries and ports. The Trans-Arabian pipeline in Saudi Arabia is one of the longest pipelines in the world, stretching 1719 km (1068 miles) from the eastern Saudi oil fields to the Mediterranean coast in Lebanon. That's the same as the distance along the whole west coast of the USA, from San Diego to Seattle.

 # Highwaymen of the Sahara?

Caravans crossing the Sahara used to travel in fear of attack from a nomadic people called the Tuareg. Tuareg men carried iron lances and double-edged swords. They wrapped their heads with long scarves coloured with a bright blue dye that rubbed off on the skin, earning them the nickname 'blue men'. Many Tuareg were traders themselves, or controlled and taxed the trade routes that passed through their lands. In the 1400s they elected a sultan to organize all their trading activities, including the collection of taxes and duties. At times the Tuareg took taxes by force, which gained them a reputation for being fierce highwaymen. Arab traders fostered this reputation to scare others off the profitable trade routes.

The Tuareg are still expert desert travellers, and they have many words for the different kinds of sand dunes and the fierce winds of the Sahara. The Tuareg men on the right are riding their camels through Algeria.

Deserts are also rich in minerals, including copper, gold, silver, phosphates, **nitrates**, zinc and precious stones. For a long time, the Atacama Desert in Chile was the world's main source of nitrates, which are used to make fertilizers and explosives. In the late 19th century, the nitrates caused war to break out between Ecuador and Chile, who both claimed the right to the mines.

In addition to mining, some countries are carrying out expensive programs to transform barren desert lands into fertile farmland. Water for the crops is usually pumped from deep underground or carried by long pipelines from elsewhere in the country. Israel has undertaken many such projects in the arid Negev Desert in the south of the country. Supplies of water from northern Israel and a year-round abundance of sunlight help produce bumper crops of vegetables, fruits and grains. But projects like this can sometimes damage the environment.

In the 1950s, the Soviet government of Turkmenistan built the Kara-Kum Canal. The canal carried water hundreds of miles from the Amu Dar'ya River to the parched Kara-Kum, enabling local people to grow cotton. An unforeseen effect, however, was the shrinking of the Aral Sea, the once vast lake into which the Amu Dar'ya flows.

Desert peoples today

Today, many nomads have abandoned the nomadic way of life and settled in cities and towns. Two-thirds of Australia's Aborigines, for example, now live in towns.

People are settling in towns for all sorts of reasons. Life in the desert can be very hard, and many desert people think their children will have better opportunities if they go to school and study, instead of learning to herd animals. Other people are simply attracted by

The fate of the San

The San people of southern Africa once roamed freely across the Kalahari Desert. They were skillful hunters with detailed knowledge of their land, and knew exactly where to find water holes or the plants and trees they needed for food, clothes and shelter.

After Europeans arrived in southern Africa in the 17th century, they named the San 'bushmen' or 'hottentots' and thought them little different from wild animals. They took their lands, enslaved many and even killed them for sport. The settlers completely exterminated one group of San, the Khoikhoi.

Over the years, the governments of southern African countries have forced the San people to settle in villages, and many now work as cattle hands or tourist guides. Today, some San are among the poorest people in southern Africa. Nevertheless, many San continue to keep their ancestral traditions alive – at least on a part-time basis. After work, men often go hunting together, though they might now wear T-shirts and jeans. The women, too, practice traditional crafts, such as beadwork and leatherwork, making objects they can sell to bring in extra income.

the hustle and bustle of city life, or the chance to get rich. In some cases, governments have forced nomadic people to settle because their independent, border-crossing lifestyle means that they are not loyal to one particular country. And in other cases, big oil and gas companies have bought up and developed ancestral lands, forcing the inhabitants to go elsewhere.

But adjusting to city life can also be hard, especially for people in poor countries. Many of the Saharan Tuareg people, for example, now live in shantytowns on the outskirts of towns such as Tombouctou, in Mali. Some survive by selling souvenirs and camel rides to tourists, and many others work in offices or factories. Some Tuareg people miss their old, freer way of life, which they call *adima*, meaning 'far from the town'.

Mongolian herders – like all desert peoples – remain experts at making the best of whatever their environment has to offer. In the Gobi desert, the Mongolian herders continue to migrate from pastureland to pastureland and live in their distinctive tents, called gers or yurts. One big difference, though, is that many herders now round up their herds on motorbikes instead of on horseback.

The lack of snow in the desert does not discourage snow boarders. The ride is bumpy and short, but a lot of fun. Other adventurous desert sports include sand sledding and dune bashing in dune buggies.

Deserts are still dangerous places for the ill-prepared, but with the right equipment, tourists now have access to the hearts of arid lands. Motorized off-road vehicles, rather than camels, are often preferred by desert dwellers and tourists alike.

Gobi and Takla Makan

The cold deserts of Mongolia and China experience extreme temperatures and bitter winters as well as scant rainfall. Despite this, herders and travelling traders have crossed these deserts for thousands of years.

 ## Beasts of burden

In the Gobi and Takla Makan lives the two-humped Bactrian camel. It has the long eyelashes, large, splaying feet and closable nostrils of other camels, but it also has a long, shaggy coat to protect it from the winter cold. Most Bactrian camels are kept by people, but some herds run truly wild in remote areas of Mongolia and China. A camel's ability to lose a quarter of its body weight in water has been useful to people wanting to cross deserts. For centuries traders and their camels crossed the Gobi and Takla Makan in groups called caravans. They carried silk and spices from China to Europe. Today, camels are still useful to desert people. The camel on the right is waiting outside its owner's dwelling, a canvas and felt tent called a yurt, or ger.

The Gobi is dominated by vast, treeless wastes. Its grey-brown surface is sparsely covered with hardy grass and bushes. Here, sand dunes dwarf a pair of yurts.

Map labels: Karakorum, 7, MONGOLIA, N, 3, 6, Altai Shan (mountains), Yelyn Valley, 8, Erenhot, Bogda Feng, Ürümqi, Turpan Depression, 5, Turpan, Gobi, Gansu Desert, 4, Lop Nur, Konqi River, CHINA, Ala Shan desert, Yellow River (Huang He), 9, Baotou, Hohhot, Altun Shan (mountains), Altun Shan, Tengger desert, Wuhai, Mu Us desert, Datong, Yinchuan, Muztag Feng, Plateau

0 100 miles
0 300 km

1. Tarim Basin
This region lies in the rain shadow of towering mountains on three sides, and very little rain reaches it. Around the rim, some rivers flow. They are fed by groundwater welling up and by snow melting on the mountains.

2. Hotan
In ancient times, merchants stayed here while travelling on the Silk Road, the major trade route from China to Europe.

3. Dzungarian Basin
Where Przewalski's horses, the last truly wild horses, roamed until the 1960s.

4. Lop Nur salt marsh
The Konqi River evaporates away in the desert sun, creating this salty marshland.

5. Turpan Depression
The lowest-lying and hottest place in China, with a record temperature of 47°C (117°F).

6. Altai Shan
A mountain refuge of the endangered snow leopard.

7. Karakorum
Warlord Genghis Khan's capital, from which he controlled a huge empire in the 13th century.

8. Yelyn Valley
A national park whose craggy cliffs are home to vultures.

9. Yellow River (Huang He)
This great river skirts the edge of the Gobi and irrigates a large area of farmland. Inside its wide meander is a further, smaller desert, the Mu Us, or Ordos.

Gobi facts

▲ There are hardly any roads in the Gobi, but the bare rock and gravel terrain is often so flat and even that you can drive a car for long distances in any direction.

▲ Some large mammals scrape a living in the Gobi, including the two-humped Bactrian camel, the Asiatic wild ass and the Mongolian gazelle.

▲ The Takla Makan desert is mainly covered in windblown sand. In the eastern foothills of the Tian Shan mountains, the sand dunes reach heights of 200–300 metres (650–1000 ft) – as tall as the Eiffel Tower in Paris.

The future for deserts

Earth's climate has been changing throughout history, and it will continue to change. Deserts naturally expand and shrink, and even disappear.

With enough irrigation, we can transform deserts. Developers built this golf course near Las Vegas, Nevada.

Algeria is now a desert country, but it was not always so. In the centre of Algeria, near a place called Aouinet, there are caves where people lived about 5500 years ago. The cave dwellers decorated their walls with paintings of everyday activities. These showed them herding cattle and hunting hippopotamuses from canoes. Some of the pictures are even earlier. They show buffalo, elephants and rhinoceroses. Clearly, the Sahara was not a desert then.

Thousands of years from now, the Sahara might be forest again, and all deserts might be different. But what about the near future?

Global warming

Many scientists think the world's climates will grow warmer during the 21st century because of the greenhouse effect. In a warmer world, rainfall might increase in what are now dry countries. If scientists are right, some present-day deserts might disappear and new ones might form. The Sahara, the Thar Desert in India and the deserts of south-west Asia could vanish altogether. The Australian deserts would not disappear, though, because they are caused partly by their distance from the ocean. But they might get smaller. Before long, livestock would be able to graze in what are now barren wastelands. And once a layer of soil had formed, farmers could begin to grow wheat and other cereal crops.

New and old deserts

In other places, life might become more difficult for people. Parts of the central USA and southern Europe could become drier – they could turn into new deserts. However, warming can also lead in some

The greenhouse effect

Some gases in the atmosphere, such as carbon dioxide, act a bit like the glass windows of a greenhouse. They let the sun's warmth pass in, but they trap the heat rays coming from the sun-warmed ground. Our cars and factories belch out extra quantities of these greenhouse gases. The increased greenhouse gases could make Earth's climate warm up unusually quickly over the next 100 years, with unpredictable effects. Although some countries would get warmer, others might get wetter, stormier or perhaps even colder. For instance, global warming could disrupt the ocean currents that keep Europe's climate mild, and Great Britain might become as cold as northern Canada.

If global warming continues, deserts in the USA could expand. Semi-arid prairie could become as dry as the scene below.

places to more evaporation, more clouds and wetter conditions. In these places, farming conditions would improve.

The west-coast deserts, such as the Namib and Atacama, will probably remain much as they are now – unless there is a big change in the circulation of the oceans. Some scientists fear that warmer air and increased rainfall might alter the ocean currents. If that were

 # Desertification

Some dry lands are not deserts, since they receive enough rainfall to support dry scrub or grassland. Herdspeople graze their animals on the grassland, but the grazing is in short supply. Particularly in dry years, overgrazing happens: animals strip the leaves from shrubs and eat grass right down to the ground. The baked, dry soil, stripped of its protective plant covering, blows away in clouds of dust. The soil can no longer support the scrubby plants, and the land becomes a desert. This process, termed desertification, is caused not only by overgrazing. It can also happen when people divert rivers elsewhere as part of an irrigation project, for instance. Desertified land cannot recover unless people return its water supply and reduce the number of grazing animals.

In some desert locations, such as Jabal Tuwayq (above) in Saudi Arabia, people draw water from deep underground to irrigate crops. The crops grow in circles because they are watered by a pivoting sprinkler. The circular fields can be more than 1.6 km (1 mile) across.

to happen, the cold currents flowing along the west coasts of the continents might weaken, allowing a layer of warm water to form above them. The Atacama and Sonoran deserts might then become wet and stormy.

If a desert changes into fertile pasture or cropland, or if farmland turns into desert, then the lives of the people living there will alter dramatically. They will have to learn new skills. Travelling nomads might have to become farmers, while farmers elsewhere might be forced to abandon their dusty fields and find other places to live.

Farming the desert

If the climate does change, there are ways to prevent farmland from turning into desert. Trees planted in lines can shield land from the wind so that the ground dries more

slowly and is less likely to get buried by dust and sand. Crops can be grown between lines of trees, and leaves from the trees can be fed to livestock. This is called corridor farming.

Rain in the desert is often so heavy that it washes soil off hillsides, but people can stop this from happening by building low walls from the stones that are common in rocky deserts. The stone walls stop mud from running straight downhill and allow soil to build up behind the walls.

In dry parts of the USA, people have figured out a system of dry farming. After a crop has been harvested, the field is left bare but ploughed occasionally to kill and bury any weeds. After three years, the rotting

weeds have nourished the soil enough for a new crop to be sown. It is even possible to grow trees on the slopes of a sand dune. First a coating of oil and rubber is sprayed on the dune to bind sand grains together. Then tree seedlings are planted through holes in the coating. Certain species of eucalyptus and acacia trees are particularly suitable – they can grow where less than 150 mm (6 in) of rain falls every year.

The soil in many desert areas is too salty for most crop plants, but certain plants, such as date palms and some varieties of almond tree, can tolerate a lot of salt. Some hardy plants, such as glasswort and sea blite, can even be watered with

Sahara resources

People use the dry lands around the fringes of the Sahara for grazing sheep, goats and cattle. Beyond the desert, on the Mediterranean coast, the climate is wet enough to grow olives, oranges and lemons. Farmers use the well-watered, fertile Nile Valley for growing a range of crops. The heart of the desert is mainly empty, but there are occasional oases where people harvest dates.

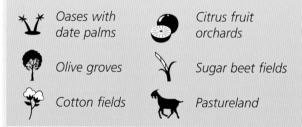

Oases with date palms		Citrus fruit orchards
Olive groves		Sugar beet fields
Cotton fields		Pastureland

seawater. Farm animals will eat some of these plants, and others can be processed to make industrial materials, such as oils.

Desert peoples

Until recently, many of the world's deserts and semi-deserts were home to nomads. But the nomadic way of life is now disappearing quickly. A dramatic change has already happened in the Persian Gulf, where large, modern cities sprang up in the desert after oil was discovered. Many of the residents now enjoy a lifestyle that their grandparents couldn't have imagined.

Similar changes are happening throughout the world's deserts, though less quickly. The Sahel is a wide band of dry grassland and scrub along the southern edge of the Sahara. Governments of countries in the Sahel have encouraged the nomadic people there to settle. The governments drilled bore holes to bring water from deep underground, and provided better veterinary care. People now keep many more animals and graze them continuously around their villages. This new lifestyle is risky because when droughts happen, the herdspeople cannot move on to graze their animals elsewhere. The animals overgraze the land, and famine may follow.

Most deserts are remote from large cities and major roads. With mobile phones, radio and TV, however, desert people know what is happening beyond the desert and can keep in touch. In years to come, as more people gain access to the Internet, they will become even more integrated into the global community.

The Great Manmade River

The country of Libya in northern Africa is made up almost entirely of desert, and most Libyans live in a thin, fertile strip of land along the coast of the Mediterranean Sea. Even on the coast, however, there is barely enough rain to plant crops and graze cattle, and drought is common.

Far beneath the blazing-hot surface of the Libyan Desert is a vast reservoir of water, trapped in a layer of absorbent rock. Much of this water trickled down thousands of years ago, before the Sahara became a desert. The Libyan government has now begun a huge project – the Great Manmade River Project – to tap the water and pump it to coastal cities. More than 200 gigantic wells will be built in the Sahara, with a combined depth of 620 km (385 miles) – seventy times the height of Mount Everest.

The future

No one knows what the world will be like a century from now. The predictions of climate change that you see on TV are based on calculations made by climatologists (scientists who study climates), but these experts seldom mention how uncertain their calculations are. And while some climatologists think that climate change will be disastrous, others think the world will warm only a tiny amount.

The future for the deserts is uncertain. Some may expand and others may shrink or vanish. Perhaps new deserts will appear. We need to learn much more about the way the world's climate works before we can forecast the weather for decades to come.

Since deserts are often sparsely populated and have very little farmland, they are good places for generating energy from new sources. Wind and solar energy are both in good, ever-renewable supply. This desert wind farm converts wind energy into electricity.

Glossary

acacia type of tree or shrub, common in semi-deserts of Africa and Australia, that often has small leaflets and thorns

amphibian cold-blooded animal that spends part of its life in water and part on land, such as a frog or salamander

aquifer large supply of water trapped deep underground

arid having a very dry climate. Deserts are arid.

atmosphere layer of air around Earth

Bedouin nomadic Arabs who live in the deserts of south-west Asia and North Africa

biome major division of the living world, distinguished by its climate and wildlife. Tundra, desert and temperate grasslands are examples of biomes.

camouflage natural disguise that makes animals or plants look like their surroundings

caravan line of vehicles or pack animals travelling together through difficult terrain

carbon dioxide gas released when fuel burns. Carbon dioxide is one of the main gases causing global warming.

climate pattern of weather that happens in one place during an average year

cold-blooded having a body temperature that depends on the surroundings. Reptiles are cold-blooded, for example. *See also* warm-blooded.

desert place that receives less than 250 mm (10 in) of rain a year

desertification process of becoming desertlike. It can happen naturally or because of human interference.

domestic animal animal kept by people, usually as a pet, farm animal or pack animal

dormant so inactive as to appear lifeless. Plant seeds often stay dormant until their soil gets wet.

ephemeral plant with a very short life cycle that appears only occasionally, such as a desert poppy

equator imaginary line around Earth, midway between the poles

evaporate to turn from liquid into gas. When water evaporates, it becomes an invisible part of the air.

excretion removal by animals or plants of chemical wastes from inside their cells

fertile capable of sustaining plant growth. Farmers often try to make soil more fertile when growing crops.

global warming gradual warming of Earth's climate, thought to be caused by pollution of the atmosphere

ice age period in history when Earth's climate was cooler and the polar ice caps expanded. The last ice age ended about 10,000 years ago.

irrigation use of channelled water by people to grow plants in dry areas

migration long-distance journey by an animal to find a new home. Many animals migrate each year.

nitrate mineral that helps plants grow

nomad person who travels from place to place in search of food and water, instead of settling permanently

oasis area where there is enough water to sustain plants, but is surrounded by desert

polar desert main biome in Antarctica, northernmost Canada and Greenland. Polar desert gets very little rain or snow, and the ground is usually barren or covered with ice.

pollination transfer of pollen from the male part of a flower to the female part of the same flower or another flower, causing the flower to produce seeds

prairie large area of grassland in central North America

predator animal that catches and eats other animals

rainforest lush forest that receives frequent heavy rainfall. Tropical rainforests grow in the tropics; temperate rainforests grow in cooler places.

rain shadow area where rainfall is low because nearby mountains provide shelter from rain-bearing winds

salt flat flat area covered with salt left behind by evaporation

salt pan natural depression in which water collects and evaporates, leaving behind salt

semi-arid having a dry climate, but not as dry as a desert. Semi-arid areas receive about 250–510 mm (10–20 inches) of rain a year.

semi-desert dry area that is not as dry as a desert. Semi-desert is most common around the fringes of deserts.

shrubland biome that mainly contains shrubs, such as the chaparral of California

species particular type of organism. Cheetahs are a species, for instance, but birds are not, because there are lots of different bird species.

succulent plant with juicy, fleshy tissue. Cacti are succulents.

taiga biome in northern regions that mainly contains conifer trees

temperate between the warm tropics and the cold, polar regions

temperate forest biome of the temperate zone that mainly contains broadleaf trees

temperate grassland biome of the temperate zone that mainly contains grassland. The US prairie is part of the temperate grassland biome.

tropic of Cancer imaginary line around Earth about 2600 km (1600 miles) north of the equator. From here, the sun appears directly overhead at noon on 21 June.

tropic of Capricorn imaginary line around Earth about 2600 km (1600 miles) south of the equator. From here, the sun is directly overhead at noon on 21 December.

tropical between the tropics of Cancer and Capricorn. Tropical countries are warm all year.

tropical forest forest growing in Earth's tropical zone, such as tropical rainforest or monsoon forest

tropical grassland tropical biome that mainly contains grassland, such as savanna

tundra biome of the far north, made up of treeless plains covered with small plants

warm-blooded having a constantly warm body temperature. Mammals and birds are warm-blooded.

water vapour gas that forms when water evaporates

Further research

Books
MacKintosh, Graham. *Into a Desert Place*. London: Harper Collins, 1988.
MacMahon, James A. *Deserts (Audubon Society Nature Guide)*. London: Random House, 1988.
MacQuitty, Miranda. *Eyewitness Desert*. London: Dorling Kindersley, 2000.
Palin, Michael. *Sahara*. London: BBC Audio, 2002.
Parker, Steve and Harris, Nathaniel. *Atlas of the World's Deserts*. London: Fitzroy Dearborn, 2002

Websites
Cool Planet: http://www.oxfam.org.uk/coolplanet/ontheline/ explore/nature/deserts/deserts.htm
(Lots of hard facts about deserts.)
Central Asian Deserts: http://www.un-mongolia.mn/wildher/greatgobi.htm
(Information from Mongolia about the Great Gobi.)
Living Edens: http://www.pbs.org/edens/
(A look at the Namib, Canyonlands, Etosha.)

Index

Page numbers in *italics* refer to picture captions.

Aborigines 46, 47, 52
acacia trees 22, 23, *47*, 59
agaves 23, 27
Al Azizia 10, 16
Anasazi civilization 47
antelopes 34–35
Arabian Desert 7, 49, 51
Arica 14
Asia
   desert animals 38–39
   desert people 47–48
Atacama 6, *7*, 18–19, *19*
   climate 14, 16–17, 58
Australia
   Aborigines 46, 47, 52
   animals 40

Bedouin 46, 47
Berbers 49, 51
birds 23, 38, 40
bristlecone pines 21

cacti 8, 22–24, *22*, 27, 28
   flowers *29*
   storing water 23
camels 34, 35, 46, 47–48
   Bactrian 35, 54, 55
cities *44*, 60
cliff dwellings 47
coastal deserts 13–14, 16–17
   see also Atacama; Namib Desert
creosote bushes 21, 26, 27–28

Death Valley 15, 16
desertification 58
domestic animals 48, 58
dust devils 12
dust storms 12, *13*

euphorbias 23, *24*, 27
explorers 48, 49

farming 52, 58–59, *58*
fennecs (foxes) 36, 42
flowers 29, *29*
fog 16, 17, *30*
food 27, 46, *47*

geckos 36
gerenuks 33–34
gila monsters 8
global warming 57, *57*
Gobi 7, 13, 54–55
   climate 12, 13
   people 53
grasses 27
grassland 5, *5*, 60
Great Basin 6, *7*, 15, 17
greenhouse effect 57
ground squirrels 36
guano 18, 30

insects 30, 34
irrigation 50, 56, 58, 59–60

jerboas 36, 39
Joshua trees 25, 26

Kalahari Desert 7, 30–31
   people 46, 52
   plants 20, 27
kangaroo rats 35
Kara-Kum, desert 7, 24, 27

Libyan Desert 61
living stones 28, *28*
lizards 39, 40

mesquite trees 22
minerals 52
Mojave Desert 25, 26
mummies 18

Namib Desert *7*, *10*, 11, 30–31
   animals 30, *32*, *37*
   climate 14, 17, 30, *30*,
   plants 20, 21, 22, 28
nomads 46–48, 52, 53

oases 49–51
oil and gas 51, 60
Okavango Delta 30, 31
oryx *13*, *32*, *37*
overgrazing 34, 58, 60

Patagonia *7*, 17, *17*
polar deserts 6, 10

quiver trees 20, *20*

railways 48–49
rain 11, *12*, 14, *14*, 16
rain shadows 17
reptiles 38–40
Riyadh 51
Romans, ancient 34

sagebrush 27
Sahara *7*, 12, 42–43
   animals 40, 42
   caravans 48
   resources 60
   settlements 60
   temperature 10, 11
   Tuareg people 51, 53
   wells 61
Sahel 60
salt flats 15

sand dunes 41, 55
sandstorms 12, *13*
San people 46, *46*, 52
saxaul trees 24, 27
scorpions *34*
shrimps 40, *40*
Sinagua people 47
Siwa 49, 51
snakes 36, 39, 41
Sonoran Desert 6, 7, *7*, 8–9, 17
   plants *23*, *26*, 29
spadefoot toads 33
spiders 41
succulents 23
Swakopmund 14

Takla Makan, desert *7*, 12, 13, 54–55
temperature 10–12, 14
transport 48–49, 55
Tuareg 51, 53
tulips 23–24, *24*

villages 49

Welwitschia plants 21, 22
west-coast deserts 17, 58
whirlwinds 12
wind farms *61*
window plant 28
winds 12, *13*
witchety grubs 46, *47*

yucca 33, *34*
yucca moth 33, *34*

Picture credits

Key: l – left, r – right, m – middle, t – top, b – bottom. **Ardea**: 24b; John Canaclosi 8b, 23b; Thomas Dressler 41; Francois Gohier 1, 15, 16b, 25, 36b, 54; Ken Lucas 34t; Stefan Meyers 32; Peter Steyn 27; M. Watson 7m, 11; C. Weaver 48; Alan Weaving 24t; Wardene Weisser 23t; **Art Explosion**: 13t, 29 (inset), 29t; **Bruce Coleman**: Jules Cowan 16t; Jeff Foott 6m, 29; Carol Hughes 37; Joe McDonald 40b; Rod Williams 39b; **Corbis**: Yann Arthus-Bertrand 30, 56 (inset), 59; Dean Conger 7r, 55; Richard Cummins 47b; Michael and Patricia Fogden 34b, 36t; Gallo Images 13m; **Image Bank**: Jean AEF Duboisberranger 45b, 53b; Frans Lemmens 7r, 43, 51; Ben Weaver 53m; **NASA**: 10, 45t, 58t; **NHPA**: A.N.T. 40t; A.N.T./Grant Dixon 6r, 19; Anthony Bannister 28, 46, 52b; Nigel J. Dennis 21b, 58b; Douglas Dickins 50; Patrick Fagot 21; Daniel Heuclin 42; John Shaw 47t; Karl Switak 33; **PhotoDisc**: Neil Beer 35; Robert Glusic 4m, 22, 56–57, 61; Bruce Heinemann 5l; Jack Hollingsworth 5m; Photolink 5r, 8t; Karl Weatherly 4r; **South American Pictures**: Chris Sharp 18. **Title page**: Ardea, Francois Gohier; **Front cover**: Corbis, Yann Arthus-Bertrand; NHPA, Daniel Heuclin (inset).